"AN EXCELLENT VOLUME"

"I welcome the book and would recommend it without hesitation to any couple contemplating marriage or already married, and that goes not only for the recently married but for the couples who have lived together in apparent harmony."

—L. Arden Almquist, M.D.

"SEXUAL HAPPINESS IN MARRIAGE has stepped in to fill a gap long obvious in our literature. This book has a number of advantages over most of the offerings presently available.

"IT IS FRANK. If you do not appreciate candor in sex discussion, this book is not for you. But if you want the plain unvarnished facts straight from the shoulder, here they are.

"THE PRESENTATION IS SPECIFIC AND PRACTICAL. Sexual relations are portrayed as an art."

—Dr. John W. Drakeford
Professor of Psychology and Counseling

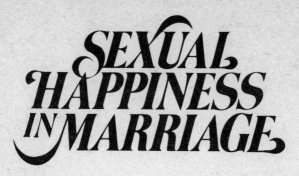

SEXUAL HAPPINESS IN MARRIAGE

A Christian Interpretation of Sexual
Adjustment in Marriage

Herbert J. Miles, Ph.D.

Illustrations by
R. EARL CLEVELAND

Revised Edition

ZONDERVAN PUBLISHING HOUSE
OF THE ZONDERVAN CORPORATION
GRAND RAPIDS, MICHIGAN 49506

*Dedicated to
one hundred and fifty-one college couples
who
requested pre-marriage counseling
and who
by courageously filling in research questionnaires after
marriage showed their faith in me and their concern
for Christian family progress*

SEXUAL HAPPINESS IN MARRIAGE
© 1967, 1976 Zondervan Publishing House

Zondervan Publishing House edition published March 1967
Zondervan Books edition published August 1969
Twenty-fifth printing   January 1978

Library of Congress Cataloging in Publication Data

Miles, Herbert Jackson, 1907-
  Sexual happiness in marriage.
  Bibliography: p.
  1. Sex in marriage.   I. Title.
[HQ31. M63   1976]   261.8'34'18   76-29620
ISBN 0-310-29202-6

Printed in the United States of America

CONTENTS

APPENDICES

FOREWORD

Pastors and Christian counselors are often called on for help regarding a Christian interpretation of sexual adjustment in marriage. This volume approaches this important subject reverently and helpfully. The author is Professor of Sociology at Carson-Newman College and has a distinctly Christian frame of reference for this writing by virtue of having earned a Master of Theology degree from Southwestern Baptist Theological Seminary.

For both engaged couples and married people even in these times, there still prevails a heavy cloud of ignorance and misunderstanding concerning the Christian meaning of sex in marriage. Need for such a manual, designed to help people from a distinctively Christian perspective, has been frequently expressed. This carefully researched volume will be welcomed both by Christian leaders in the counseling role and by Christian couples who feel the need for specific help regarding the sexual aspects of marriage.

Any Christian couple must gauge the fulfillment of their sexual relationship to each other, of course, by no artificial standard of excellence but by the meeting of their mutual needs within basic, God-given boundaries. In a unique way, this marriage manual is designed to help thoughtful Christian people from all walks of life. I hope it will contribute materially to the current search for a better understanding of the Christian meaning of sex.

FOY VALENTINE, *Executive Secretary Christian Life Commission of the Southern Baptist Convention 1966*

PREFACE to the Second Edition

This book is addressed to four groups: (1) engaged couples preparing for marriage; (2) married couples who may be having some sex problems; (3) married couples who would like to keep their love life fresh and growing; and (4) pastors, church staff members, denominational leaders, and lay religious leaders who are frequently involved in some type of sexual counseling. It is an effort to help these groups gain Biblical insight, develop realistic attitudes, and make Christian value-judgments concerning sexual adjustment in marriage. In the past, traditional myths have corroded the thinking, distorted the perspectives, and undermined the motivation of church-related people concerning sex in human life. It is hoped that the readers will be challenged (1) to think concerning God's plan for sex in marriage; (2) to reexamine their own (often traditional) assumptions; and (3) to relate what is learned to their own sexual motivations, decisions, and behavior patterns.

The original manuscript was completed in April of 1966. During the last ten years much scientific data resulting from research and marriage counseling experience have been established. Every effort has been made to bring this book up-to-date by reflecting the present-day thinking of family-life specialists. In the last ten years there has been a major ground swell in the matter of sex education by most Christian groups, both in precept and actual practice. This sex-education advance has been clothed in the framework of a special emphasis on family life in the form of denominational literature, church family-life conferences, and pastoral and lay pre-marriage and marriage counseling. This has been true in all evangelical denominations (both large and small), including their seminaries, Bible schools, colleges, and universities. For example, this nationwide movement is reflected in the Continental Congress on Family Life which met in St. Louis in October 1975. More than 2,200 persons attended from over fifty denominations from all fifty states and six foreign nations. Also, hundreds of denominational and interdenominational family-life conferences are being held annually on the county, district, state, and regional levels. Dozens of new books on marriage and family life are being published by evangelical publishing houses annually. This interest and advance in family life by the evangelical world calls for a revision of this book.

Minor changes have been made throughout the book reflecting new empirical data that have surfaced during the past ten years. Some major changes involving new materials have been made in chapters 5, 6, and 7. Appendix IV, "A Selected Bibliography," has been completely rewritten. Some older books have been deleted, and many books written in the last two or three years have been added.

I have been teaching, counseling, lecturing, and holding church family-life conferences for the past twenty-eight years. From this total experience, impressions have been gained and insights achieved that I hope will contribute at least some degree of validity to what I have written.

HERBERT J. MILES
Professor Emeritus of Sociology
Carson-Newman College
April 1976

PREFACE to the First Edition

For many generations, the churches of the Christian community have left sexual training to other persons and groups in society. The medical doctor has generally been accepted as the best authority in matters pertaining to sex. Medical scientists have been determined to conquer the physical diseases of the human body. They have been extremely successful in their efforts. Yet there seems to be some evidence that in their necessary preoccupation with physical diseases they have somewhat neglected the sexual aspect of human life. In the meantime, our society has become more aware of the fact that sex is not just a physical something. Sex is physical, but at the same time, it is a spiritual, emotional, mental, social something. Medical science does speak with authority on the physical aspects of sex. But the other aspects of sex are largely outside of the basic area of responsibility assumed by medical science.

As a result of this increased awareness of the non-physical aspects of sex, a new group of specialists in human behavior has appeared on the scene during the last two decades. They have taken the leadership in matters related to sex life. These specialists include marriage counselors, psychologists, sociologists, social workers, pastors, and psychiatrists. They have made substantial progress in promoting normal sex life in marriage. This is especially true of the American Association of Marriage and Family Counselors which has furnished the organized leadership to spearhead this major social transition. It is obvious that the complexity of human behavior and the problems involved make this new division of labor necessary. During this transition, sociological and psychological research, in cooperation with a secular cultural drift, has brought the subject of sex out into the open where it is discussed publicly and freely.

In this transition, a basic problem has arisen. This problem is not that sex is now considered a legitimate subject for research. Neither is it the fact that specialists are giving guidance on sexual matters. Rather, the basic problem is the fact that the communications system and many other vested interest groups are exploiting sex for economic gain. Also, many individual quacks, charlatans, and other boastful pretenders are exploiting sex for quick money and for selfish gratification. This exploitation has muddied the waters. Basically, it has been a frontal attack upon the historic Christian concepts of marriage and sexuality. As a result of this, many thousands of adults and youth are confused and frustrated with regard to the meaning, function, and purpose of their sexual nature.

Because of this basic problem, growing out of the social transition of the past two decades, the Christian community has launched a sizeable counterattack. The backbone of this counterattack has been the writing of many articles, pamphlets, and books by able Christian leaders which are designed to set forth the creative plan of God for sexuality in marriage, in the family, and in the community (see Appendix IV). Most of these writings are of excellent quality and are fully in line with the mainstream of the missionary redemptive program of modern New Testament Christianity. These authors rightly assume that redeemed Christian leaders are in a superior position to understand and interpret the purpose of sex in the creative plan of God.

The main weakness of this counterattack up to now, is that we have not gone far enough. We have been largely theoretical, talking in accurate and beautiful language about God and sex. But we have failed at the precise point of applying these theoretical concepts to real life situations in the area of pre-marriage training and counseling. To date, there has not been a single book published in a positive Christian and Biblical frame of reference, which gives the details of the attitudes and techniques necessary for good sexual adjustment in marriage. All of the manuals on sexual adjustment in marriage have been secular, that is, they have not been written from a definite, explicit Christian point of view. We propose that pastors and other Christian counselors apply our Christian theory of sex to real life situations. We recommend that churches, pastors, and other Christian leaders assume the responsibility for adequate pre-marriage counseling in the area of sexual adjustment in marriage.

This book is to encourage the next logical step in the counterattack. The ascetic standards of the past need to be replaced by Christian standards. We need to talk plainly in sincere, frank, concrete language. We must claim sex within marriage for Christianity. We must relate the wonderful gift of sex to the purposes of God. It is God's intention for His people (not Satan's) to know the fullest satisfaction in every area of the present created order.

In the chapters ahead, the discussion of sexual adjustment in marriage revolves around four ideas: (1) Christian theory, (2) proper attitudes, (3) proper techniques, and (4) factual data from the author's current research. Chapter 1 gives the background and approach to the study of sexuality in marriage. Chapter 2 is a presentation of Christian and Biblical attitudes and teachings concerning sex. Chapter 3 presents a brief description of male and female reproductive and sexual organs and their functions. Chapters 4 and 5 give the basic techniques involved in order to achieve good sexual adjustment in marriage. Chapter 6 discusses planned parenthood through the use of contraceptives. Chapter 7 deals with the causes of inadequate sexual adjustment.

Appendix I describes the research methods used in our study of the sexual adjustment of 151 couples who had been given pre-marriage counseling. Appendix II contains the research questionnaire with the tabulated results in the form of percentages and averages. Appendix III outlines some specific suggestions which pastors and other church leaders may use in a planned church program of pre-marriage training and counseling. Appendix IV is a selected list of books, pamphlets, and literature that may assist churches to secure further help and supplies. Appendix V gives information on how to locate a qualified marriage counselor.

I am indebted to dozens of people who have made many contributions to the writing of this book. This indebtedness is gratefully acknowledged. Also, I am thankful for my teachers, T. B. Maston, H. E. Dana, W. T. Conner, Olin T. Binkley, and Wayne E. Oates who gave me practical theological and sociological foundations which have been exceedingly helpful in developing a workable theory for marriage and family life. A large number of contemporary scholars who have spearheaded the current movement to claim sex for Christianity have also helped. The writing and lectures of David Mace, Paul Popenoe, Judson Landis, C. W. Scudder, Lofton Hudson, Peter A. Bertocci, Otto A. Piper, Sylvanus M. Duvall, and Evelyn Mills Duvall have been a continual inspiration to me.

I am deeply indebted to the following who assisted

me in formulating the research project and questionnaire and/or read parts or all of the manuscript and made many valuable suggestions: Prof. Ray F. Koonce, psychologist and counselor; Dr. Gary E. Farley, sociologist; Dr. Nat C. Bettis, Bible teacher; Dr. Wade E. Darby, clergyman; Dr. William E. Crane, marriage counselor; Dr. Olin T. Binkley, seminary president; Dr. J. B. Sams, physician and surgeon; Dr. Robert Zondervan, psychiatrist; Mrs. Audra Trull, pastor's wife; Mrs. Jacqueline Farley, registered nurse; and Mrs. Betty H. Cleveland, registered nurse.

I am indebted to eleven Carson-Newman senior sociology majors and minors, Roy Ellis, Charles Jones, Tom Bailey, Bill Amos, Bob Landes, Eddie Blount, Rick Teal, William Gillett, Glen Grubb, Vernon Johnston, and Charles Kratz, who assisted me in our sociological research laboratory.

I am grateful to six secretaries, Mrs. Delores Ellis, Mrs. Jean Billington, Mrs. Harriet Blount, Mrs. Ruth Givins, Mrs. Joyce Smith, and Mrs. Becky Teague who gave careful attention to the preparation of both the research and the manuscript. I am humbly grateful for my wife who read the manuscript several times and made many valuable suggestions. I cannot adequately put into words my heartfelt appreciation for her insight, sympathy, and understanding.

HERBERT J. MILES
Professor of Sociology
Carson-Newman College
April 1966

CHAPTER 1

Sex the Servant of Christianity

JIM, A COLLEGE senior, stopped me in the corridor between classes and asked if he could talk to me privately. When we were alone, he told me that he was planning to be married soon after graduation, which was only a few weeks away. He said that he wanted to have a conference with some member of the faculty. Hesitating briefly, he then added, "I want to talk to someone about the physical relationships between husband and wife in marriage." Then with a smile and with confidence he said, "I have studied the list of the college faculty in the catalog and I have selected you as the one I want to talk with."

He was a ministerial volunteer and an honor roll student who had been elected to high office by the student body. His outgoing personality was characterized by maturity, dignity, kindness, and friendliness.

He was engaged to one of the most capable, refined, and attractive girls of the senior class. Human nature being what it is, I was extremely proud of being selected by Jim for this conference. Privately, in my mind, I reached up and straightened my halo and at the same time tried to appear humble as I accepted the invitation to talk with him. Most people seem to think of themselves as authorities on courtship, marriage, and the family. I was no exception. Although I had not had any specific conferences like this before, I knew that I would be "good."

On the day of the conference, as the two of us sat down privately to talk, he took a notebook out of his pocket and opened it. It was a small three by five spiral notebook. He began asking questions which he had written in the notebook. There were two questions on each page. They were organized by subject and were detailed. Before he had asked five questions, I realized that I had made a major mistake and that he was talking to the wrong faculty member. By that time, I knew that *he* knew that he was talking to the wrong faculty member. Being the gentleman that he was, he continued with the questions and tried not to embarrass me. He turned page after page in the little notebook asking question after question. His questions concerned sexual adjustment in marriage. The longer he continued, the more specific he became. He wanted to know about attitudes, techniques, scientific information, percentages, averages, etc., ad infinitum. In answer to his questions, I guessed, "hemmed," "hawed," and avoided. It seemed that he would never get to the end of the notebook. He must have asked fifty or sixty questions. When he finally finished, he stood up and thanked me as graciously as if he had just finished a successful conference with the governor or the president.

Although my pride would not allow me to reveal it to him, I do not recall that I have ever been so humiliated. That night I could not sleep. I could not get Jim off my mind. I asked for and received divine forgiveness for my self-centeredness and overconfidence. But I rolled and tossed on into the night. Each time I would shut my eyes and try to sleep, I could see Jim sitting directly in front of me, turning pages and asking questions. His serious, piercing eyes were looking right through me imploring positive answers. I would review the questions he asked me. Every question was intelligent. He had a right to have the answers and he deserved intelligent answers. Many ideas paraded before my mind that night. In rationalization, I mentally looked up and down the list of faculty members to decide which other member of the faculty he could have asked. After a survey, I decided that there was probably not one member of our fine faculty who was any better prepared to answer his questions than I was. Furthermore, I decided that it was intelligent for him to select me, because I was the teacher of the sociology classes in marriage and the family. The needs of this young man as he stood near the marriage altar flooded my soul.

My thinking flashed back across the years to the weeks before I married the bride of my youth. We had agreed that I should talk to a physician, which I did. The physician was reluctant to talk, and I received even less help than I had given Jim. We needed help and did not receive it. Then I thought of the twenty years while I was a pastor. I had performed many wedding ceremonies. I had given much counsel, religious and otherwise, but I had not given all of the help that those couples really needed. My college and seminary classes had given me no help at this point.

That night, like Jacob of old, I wrestled with this problem "until the break of day." I was overwhelmed by it all. My experience with Jim seemed to be saying to me, "Here is an open door. Your life experience and your present situation make you fit to enter this door." I kept asking myself, "Could it be that this is the same divine leadership that had called me into the ministry, and that had called my wife and me to serve as professors in a Christian college?" It seemed that the answer must be "Yes." Nothing else made sense: Finally, I made a positive decision and in the early part of the dawn, I fell asleep. The next day and during the days ahead, it was with confidence that a program of pre-marriage counseling came to be a positive addition to my teaching responsibilities. During the next few months I read many books on marriage counseling.

In the fall semester, I simply announced in my marriage and family classes that I was a practicing marriage counselor and that my door was open to discuss problems related to courtship, marriage, and family life. Later in the semester, in discussing specific plans for marriage, I announced that I was prepared to discuss sexual adjustment with couples who were planning marriage. Immediately, couples began to knock on my door. There followed a long line of eager, sincere young people like Jim and his bride, sincerely requesting help concerning sexual adjustment in marriage.

Eleven years and two hundred and seventy-five couples later, this book was sent forth with the prayer that it may be used to strengthen the marriage and brighten the way of many other worthy couples.

Truly, it can be said that God uses people (Jim) and personal experiences (my encounter with Jim) to open doors and to guide His followers into needy areas to speed Christian progress.

There seems to be a new concern among Christian
people of all religious groups calling for the churches,
church institutions, and church leaders to take the initiative in interpreting sex to the world, in light of the plan of
the divine Creator and basic Christian principles. The
following statements made by a recent Southern Baptist
Conference on Family Life are typical of this concern.
"Marriage is intended to meet the sexual needs of both
partners. . . . 'Southern Baptists have scarcely begun to
face our responsibility in this matter. . . .' A new climate
is required in dealing with human sexuality. Current
attitudes reflect more of the Puritan tradition than the
frankness of the Biblical approach. One's maleness or
femaleness affects his total life and relationships, not
simply his marriage and home. The Biblical view is a
needed corrective for Southern Baptist thought." Some of
the recommendations made by the conference concerning sexuality were:

1) That all Southern Baptist agencies dealing with
   marriage and home reexamine their literature,
   programs, and policies with a view to strength-
   ening their contributions in the area of Christian
   teachings on sex and marriage (p. 15).

2) That we teach the relationship of sex to the
   purposes of God (p. 22).

3) That we include a stronger emphasis in Sunday
   school and Training Union literature upon sex
   education at *all age levels*, including married
   persons (p. 23).

4) That research projects in sex education be carried out (p. 24).

5) That in premarital education, the churches have
   adequate counseling sessions by the pastor (with

couples planning marriage) . . . including sex
information (the physical side of marriage and
the attitude of each toward the physical side of
marriage) (pp. 39, 40). [1]

Almost all other denominational groups have made
similar recommendations. This new concern on the part
of Christian leaders rests upon the conviction that Christianity and sex are friends, close friends. It is believed
that sex was planned to be, can be, and must be the friend
of Christianity, not an enemy. The mainstream of Christian thought going all the way back to the Hebrews has
always placed Christianity and sex on friendly terms. Not
only is sex a friend of Christianity, but it was planned to
serve Christianity. In the plan of God, *sex is the servant
of Christianity*. A servant it must become. The time is
long overdue for the Christian community to help young
couples toward effective sexual adjustment in marriage
by seeing that they receive thorough pre-marriage training and counseling.

A Guide to Sexual Adjustment

This book is an effort in that direction and is designed to be a guide to sexual adjustment in marriage.
Designed to be used by pastors and all types of counselors, it has three major differences from standard sex
manuals now being used.

First, detailed information and instruction on how
to achieve sexual adjustment in marriage is discussed in
a Christian and Biblical frame of reference. In the past,
many pastors and other Christian counselors have had to
apologize for using manuals on sexual adjustment which
avoided positive Christian ideals.

Second, this book is the result of many years of
systematic pre-marriage counseling, followed by re-

search to measure the success of the counseling. The pre-marriage counseling and research grew out of the author's teaching Marriage and Family classes in college.

Finally, a greater emphasis is placed upon both detailed techniques and proper attitudes in sexual efforts. Alternative techniques are described and evaluated. Some writers on the subject of sex make light of books describing techniques. It is our feeling that young couples entering marriage, having had no sexual experience, have a moral and social right to be thoroughly instructed as to possible techniques, what to avoid, and what to expect. It is felt that such instruction reduces anxiety to its lowest possible level, and generally speeds success and efficiency. Our research substantiated this contention. Also, we feel that proper Christian attitudes are as significant as proper techniques, or more so. The two move together.

AN AUDIENCE OF TWO

Although this volume is planned to be used by pastors and other counselors, it is written specifically to "two audiences of two people." First, it is written to any couple who have moved through the normal processes of courtship, who are in a bona fide engagement, who have the wedding date set, and who are within three weeks to three months of their wedding day. The message of this book is directed primarily to this audience of two people. The audience should never be larger except when a qualified counselor is in charge.

Secondly, this book is addressed to Mr. and Mrs. John Q. Public. Most married couples could find some help in reading it. It should be particularly helpful to those who may not have had access to thorough pre-marriage counseling, or who may be somewhat unhappy with their sexual progress in marriage. Actually, it would be well for any husband and wife to read this volume and discuss the ideas set forth in each chapter. Such a study should help them in three ways. It would help them to understand more thoroughly the relationship of sex to the Christian life. Also, it should help them to unify and crystallize their thinking, relative to their own sexual experience, and should encourage self-confidence and progress. Finally, it should give them a source of information that would enable them to be of assistance to friends who may be planning marriage, or to married friends who may be floundering in their sexual experiences and drifting toward separation and divorce.

MATERIALISM: AN ANIMAL PHILOSOPHY

To understand the place of sex in human life, young couples entering marriage need to be acquainted with some of the extreme ideas about sex which tend to pervert it into corrupt channels. Before presenting a Christian interpretation of marriage and sexuality, it is well for us to sketch the teaching of materialism and asceticism, the two major ideas about human life that oppose the Christian point of view.

The teachings of traditional materialism, if perhaps somewhat overdrawn, are basically as follows: Material matter was the only thing in existence in the beginning. Matter is made up of chemical elements. Chemical elements are made up of atoms. Atoms are in motion. They are eternal and possess energy and power. Life is simply an unfolding of matter. All things are merely combinations of chemical elements. Mind is simply the functioning of matter. There is no creative force, no organizing agent, no purpose, no goals, no ends, no God, no life after death. Modern forms of materialism are usually watered down with cultural, social, and psychological theories. They normally avoid being labeled "materialism." However, we should not be misled. Martin H. Scharlemann points out that a materialistic psychologist "when pressed, shows that he firmly believes in the same kind of world that the traditional materialistic monist believed in, whether he is philosophically prone to apply the old label or not" *(What, Then, Is Man?* Concordia Publishing House, St. Louis, 1958, page 83). It is obvious that materialistic ideas rest only upon part truths. These ideas are out of line with and ignore much of total reality. The Apostle Paul warned, "Be careful that nobody spoils your faith through intellectualism and high sounding nonsense" (Col. 2:8, PHILLIPS).

When materialistic theories are applied to marriage and sexuality, many weird ideas evolve. Since man is essentially an animal, love is said to be nothing more than sex desire. Sex is only an expression of the flesh. Health requires that the sex desire be satisfied immediately after puberty. When a man chooses a wife, he simply selects a good sex partner. Extra-marital sex relations are normal. When sex attraction no longer exists between husband and wife, divorce is in order. There is no such thing as sexual delinquency, so long as one person does not force another. The way to solve the problem of children being born out of wedlock, is to give 13-year-old boys and girls full access to contraceptives and train them how to use them. In case there should be a pre-marriage pregnancy, abortion is advocated. Promiscuity, from puberty to old age, is encouraged. Sex is said to be a private matter. Private sexual behavior is said to be none of society's business.

It would be rather difficult to collect a greater set of

falsehoods into one system than is found in these ideas. This system advocates standard barnyard morality. Put into practice, it would take civilization back to the jungle.

ASCETICISM: A DEAD-END STREET

Whereas materialism overemphasizes the importance of the flesh and avoids or denies the spirit, the theory of asceticism rushes to the other extreme. It overemphasizes the spirit and denies the significance of the flesh as much as possible. According to ascetic ideas, matter is evil and the flesh is evil; therefore, a person must rigidly deny the expression of the flesh and of sex, in order to reach a high state of morality, intellectuality, and spirituality.

The theory of asceticism is best illustrated in the ideas taught by Mani, the founder of Manichaeism. Mani was born in Persia in A.D. 215. His teachings may be summarized as follows. The universe began by the mixing of *two* elements, "Light" and "Darkness." Light was essentially *good*. Darkness was essentially *evil*. Man and woman were made up of both Light and Darkness. Their bodies belonged to the lower elements of Dark matter. Their souls belonged to the concentrated elements of Light. The elements of Light and Darkness were at war within both man and woman. The purpose and process of world development was to release the Light from the Darkness. At the end of the world, Light would triumph over Darkness.

When Mani applied those ideas (normally called ascetic dualism) to marriage and sexuality, the result was a negative doctrine of abstinence. Since the body was made up of Darkness, it follows that the body was evil, the flesh was evil, sex was evil, and reproduction was evil. These ideas rigidly carried out and followed to their logical conclusion would soon depopulate the earth. These and other ascetic ideas originated in Greek philosophy and Persian and Oriental religions. The Hebrews of the Old Testament and Jesus and the Apostles of the New Testament were not ascetic dualists. Instead of a dualism, the Hebrew-Christian thinkers began their explanation of the universe, not with two limited beings, but with *one* free, infinite, eternal, omnipotent God.

These two extreme theories, materialism and asceticism, are evils that would pervert and destroy the Christian doctrines of marriage and sexuality. They root far back into the pages of history, certainly all the way back to the early Greek philosophers. At the same time, they are present, active and aggressive in today's world. Couples in the process of planning and living a life of Christian marriage need to be acquainted with the evil nature of these two theories in order to recognize them and reject them. When we recognize these extremes, it helps us to understand Christian ideas about marriage and sex. Whereas materialism overemphasizes the flesh and tends to deny the importance of the spirit, and whereas asceticism overemphasizes the spirit and tends to deny the importance of the flesh, the Christian doctrine brings the spirit and the flesh together to cooperate as one total unit in the life of each person. It is necessary to understand this doctrine in order to have good sexual adjustment in marriage. We now turn to the task of describing Christian and Biblical teachings concerning sexuality in marriage and family life.

Notes

[1] *The Church and the Christian Family*, Resource Book from the Southern Baptist Family Life Conference (Nashville: Family Life Department, Joe Burton, Secretary, 1963).

CHAPTER 2

A Christian Interpretation of Sex in Marriage

All scripture is inspired of God and is useful for teaching the faith and correcting error, for resetting the direction of a man's life and training him in good living.   2 Timothy 3:16 (PHILLIPS)

THE BIBLE is the record of God's revelation of Himself to man in the person of Jesus Christ. It is concerned with such ideas as sin, salvation, evangelism, missions, individual spiritual growth, a Christian social order, and eternal life. Thus, the Bible is not basically a book on science, agriculture, art, music, architecture, or sociology. Yet the Bible contains many ideas concerning these and many other topics. In a similar manner, the Bible is not a book on sex. However, it does contain many specific ideas concerning sex and how sex fits into the total plan of creation and the progress of the kingdom of God. It should be helpful to any couple planning marriage to study carefully some of the Bible passages definitely related to the place of sexuality in marriage and family life. Let us examine seven such passages.

> 1. *So God created man in his own image, in the image of God created he him, male and female created he them. And God blessed them, and said unto them "Be fruitful, and multiply, and replenish the earth and subdue it."* . . .
>
> Genesis 1:27-28

This passage indicates that God created both man and woman as complete individuals. On the non-physical side of their nature, they are persons, made in the image of God. They are personalities that are intelligent, rational, free, and accountable. On the physical side, they possess physical bodies including sexuality and the capacity to reproduce. In the command to "Be fruitful, and multiply," we have sex in the creation of man and woman for the purpose of procreation (reproduction). This is basic in the plan of God in creation.

> 2. *And therefore shall a man leave his father and his mother, and shall cleave unto his wife; and they shall be one flesh. And they were both naked, the man and his wife, and were not ashamed.*
>
> Genesis 2:24-25

The central part of this passage is the phrase "shall be one flesh." This phrase refers to the bodily and spiritual union of husband and wife in sexual intercourse. It includes a definite sexual experience (orgasms) for both husband and wife. This "one-flesh" relationship does not refer specifically to reproduction, but rather to sex as a profound personal experience of spiritual and physical pleasure between husband and wife. Many other Bible passages clearly emphasize this same concept (Gen. 24:67; Eccl. 9:9; Song of Sol.). The nature of this pleasure is at the same time both physical and spiritual. It involves the total physical body and the total mental, emotional, and spiritual nature of both husband and wife. It involves the action of the total personality. God created this one-flesh experience to be the most intense height of physical intimacy and the most profound depth of spiritual oneness between husband and wife. It is well to note that Jesus quoted this passage as a basis for His ideas about marriage (Matt. 19:4-5; Mark 10:9).

3. *And God saw everything that he had made and behold it was very good.* Genesis 1:31

When animals were created, the Genesis record states that "God saw that it was good" (Gen. 1:25). However, when God created man and woman, male and female, in His image, the Genesis record states, "Behold, it was *very* good." The meaning of this passage is that the Creator-God formed in His mind a plan to create male and female persons in His image. After the creative act, He viewed His finished product, man and woman, and they appeared to be an accurate duplicate, a perfect reproduction of His original purpose and design. What is it that is good? The "maleness" of man is very good. The "femaleness" of woman is very good. Both man and woman were created with physical reproductive bodies. At the same time, they were created spiritually in the image of God. That is, they were persons characterized by self-consciousness, self-knowledge, self-control, the ability to think, to choose, to will, etc. This total complete unit of mind and body is "very good."

4. *My son, attend unto my wisdom, and bow thine ear to my understanding.*

That thou mayest regard discretion, and that thy lips may keep knowledge.

For the lips of a strange woman drop as an honeycomb, and her mouth is smoother than oil:

But her end is bitter as wormwood, sharp as a two-edged sword.

Her feet go down to death; her steps take hold on hell.

Lest thou shouldest ponder the path of life, her ways are moveable, that thou canst not know them.

Hear me now therefore, O ye children, and depart not from the words of my mouth.

Remove thy way far from her, and come not nigh the door of her house.   Proverbs 5:1-8

And why wilt thou, my son, be ravished with a strange woman, and embrace the bosom of a stranger?   Proverbs 5:20

This passage gives strong and stern warnings to young men about the misuse of their sexual life. They are instructed not to express their sexual nature in promiscuous intercourse with loose women. Then, these exacting negative warnings are followed by beautiful positive instructions indicating how young men *should* meet their sexual needs. These instructions are as follows:

Drink waters out of thine own cistern, and running waters out of thine own well.

> *Let thy fountain be blessed: and rejoice with the*
> *wife of thy youth.*
> *Let her be as the loving hind and pleasant roe; let*
> *her breasts satisfy thee at all times; and be thou*
> *ravished always with her love.*
>
> Proverbs 5:15, 18-19

This passage in clear and distinct tones states that a young man is to meet his sexual needs in sexual intercourse with his wife. To do so will fill him with happiness, joy, and rejoicing. His wife is described as tender, gentle, beautiful, graceful, charming, and satisfying. She is referred to as his "cistern" (verse 15), his "stream of running water" (verse 15), and his "fountain" (verse 18). These three figures are symbolic of his wife as his sexual partner. Just as a person's thirst may be continually satisfied by drinking cool fresh water from a cistern, a clear running stream, or a fountain, so a man's sexual thirst should be regularly met in sexual experiences with his wife. The last part of verse 19 may be translated, "Let your wife's love and your sexual embrace with your wife intoxicate you continually with delight. Always enjoy the ecstasy of her love." Not only is a man's behavior, when he is meeting his sexual needs in marriage with his wife, represented as wisdom and intelligence (verse 1), but God is represented as always *knowing, watching,* and *approving* this relationship (verse 21). It is obvious that this entire chapter is discussing sex in marriage as a unitive pleasure between husband and wife. Procreation and children are not mentioned.

5. The clearest passage in the New Testament setting forth the basic truths of the Christian point of view on sexual adjustment in marriage is 1 Corinthians 7:2-5.

For our purposes it is helpful to give this passage the following free translation:

> *Because of the strong nature of the sexual drive, each man should have his own wife, and each woman should have her own husband. The husband should regularly meet his wife's sexual needs, and the wife should regularly meet her husband's sexual needs. In marriage, just as the wife's body belongs to her husband and he rules over it, so in marriage, the husband's body belongs to his wife and she rules over it. Do not refuse to meet each other's sexual needs, unless you both agree to abstain from intercourse for a short time in order to devote yourselves to prayer. But because of your strong sexual drive, when this short period is passed, continue to meet each other's sexual needs by coming together again in sexual intercourse.*

There are three ideas concerning sexuality that stand skyscraper tall out of this passage commanding our attention.

1) Both husband and wife have definite and equal sexual needs that should be met in marriage. The primitive idea that sex is man's prerogative and that his wife should submit to him, remain passive and silent, is not only in violation of known scientific facts about woman's sexual nature, but is also in violation of the clear teaching of this Bible passage which states in exacting language (1 Cor. 7:3), "The husband should regularly meet his wife's sexual needs." Williams translates it, "The husband must always give his wife what is due her." The passage is saying that women have a definite need for regular sexual experiences in marriage and it assumes that regular sexual orgasms in a sexual experience with

her husband are due her, and are necessary to complete the unitive nature of marriage.

2) It is not the responsibility of the husband to meet his own sexual needs, nor is it the responsibility of the wife to meet her own sexual needs. Rather it is the husband's responsibility to continually meet his wife's sexual needs and it is the wife's responsibility to continually meet her husband's sexual needs. It is a cooperative experience. In this manner, the total needs of both are continually met.

3) The fact that husband and wife enjoy meeting each other's sexual needs as life moves on in this unitive relationship does not conflict with the Hebrew-Christian concept of a devout spiritual life, such as following fully the will of God, growth in grace in Christ, Christian service, and stewardship. Rather, this Scripture implies that an efficient Christian life and an efficient sexual adjustment in marriage really go together. Note that Paul intersperses the husband and wife's sex life with their prayer life (1 Cor. 7:5).

6. 1 Thessalonians 4:1-8 (selected sentences from the RSV)

> *Finally, brethren, we beseech and exhort you in the Lord Jesus Christ that . . . you ought to live and to please God . . . For this is the will of God . . . that you abstain from immorality; that each one of you know how to take a wife for himself in holiness and in honor, not in the passion of lust like heathen who do not know God: . . . For God has not called us for uncleanness but in holiness.*

The following observations about sex in marriage seem to flow from this passage:

1) God instituted marriage and the sexual nature of marriage.

2) Each man is to select his own wife (and each woman her own husband).

3) The motive for the selection must be characterized by personal purity, concern for a total life relationship, holiness, and honor.

4) To allow sexual passions alone to guide one in selecting a wife, as pagans do, is unclean and a violation of the will of God.

5) By entering marriage the right way one performs the will of God.

These instructions are given "by the authority of the Lord Jesus" (verse 2, WILLIAMS).

7. The Song of Solomon

It is necessary to consider the Song of Solomon in order to give an adequate summary to the teaching of the Scriptures on sex life in marriage. The Song of Solomon contains eight chapters of beautiful poetry. It is poetry about the love relationships between husband and wife. It exalts fidelity between married lovers. Some Bible scholars think that it is an actual historical experience involving several persons. Others think it is a collection of wedding songs describing the spiritual happiness and the physical joys of wedlock. It may have been either or both. Regardless of the interpretation accepted, it is clear that the Song of Solomon describes pre-New Testament Jewish ideas about love and sexuality in marriage. The Song of Solomon describes in vivid poetic language the physical bodies of married lovers, and does not offend (6:1-10; 7:1-9). Techniques in sexual arousal between husband and wife are implied (2:3; 8:3). The feelings, the attitudes, the imaginations, the dreams, the spiritual joys, the sexual joys, and the romantic happinesses of married lovers are beautifully described.

There are many other passages in the Scriptures that give similar ideas about sex in marriage. In Hebrews 13:4 we are exhorted to "Let marriage be held in honor among all, and let the marriage bed be undefiled. . . ." In Exodus 20:14 the command, "Thou shalt not commit adultery," assumes a positive command, "Thou *shalt* meet thy sexual needs in marriage."

In general, the New Testament follows the Old Testament ideas about the place of sex in human life. The following New Testament passages are important examples: Matthew 5:32; Matthew 19:4-6; Mark 2:19; Mark 10:6-9; Luke 16:18; John 2:1-11; John 3:29; Romans 1:26-27; 1 Corinthians 7:9; 1 Corinthians 9:15; Ephesians 5:3-12; Ephesians 5:23-25; 1 Timothy 3:2, 12; 1 Timothy 4:3-4; 2 Timothy 2:22; Jude 7; and Revelation 19:7-9.

Many young couples entering marriage do not possess clear ideas about the relationship of sex life to basic Christian teachings. Sometimes they entertain vague ideas that sex is necessary, but somewhat "worldly." They have these ideas simply because no one has ever given them a true picture of Bible teaching on this subject. The above study of seven representative Bible passages is sufficient to guide us in setting out a broad summary outline on the positive teachings of the Bible concerning sex and marriage. Couples need some basic principles and guidelines to assist them in focusing and crystallizing their own ideas and attitudes on sexual matters into a mature and consistent whole. They need a practical workable set of principles to follow or a standard to live by. The following propositions are based on the Bible passages studied above and represent a concise summary of Christian thought on the plan and purpose of sexuality in human life. The discussion following each proposition is a short review of current Christian insights and understanding of the principle set forth in the proposition.

PROPOSITION 1.

The universe and all life is a CREATION OF GOD.

The Christian movement rests upon the simple, yet profound assumption that "In the beginning God created" all things (Gen. 1:1; Col. 1:16; Heb. 11:3). All efforts to understand and explain the world must begin with an initial idea about origins. The Christian assumption is that God existed before the universe and living things came into existence. God is Creator, Redeemer, Preserver, and Ruler of the universe. He is spiritual, personal, self-sufficient, free, intelligent, moral, and sovereign. He is infinite in all qualities. He did not make the world out of some pre-existent "stuff," nor did He make it out of Himself. He created that which did not exist.

The method used in creation is not explained in the Bible. It is simply stated, assumed. God's creation was the result of His intelligent purpose. The different parts of the whole life of His creation were related to one another. Creation was marked by order, continuity, reproductivity, law, and unity.

In general, the Christian concept of creation is that the universe came from God. The "person," the "mind," and the purposive "will" of God is the sole ground, cause, and explanation of creation. God existed first. Not only did He bring the physical and human world into existence, but it continues to depend on Him. Christians carefully avoid theories that would identify God with nature or beliefs that He created the world and withdrew, having nothing to do with it. Our ideas concerning marriage and sexuality must flow logically from this initial assumption that God created the universe and all life.

PROPOSITION 2.

God created man and woman as individual persons,
COMPOSED OF MIND AND BODY *(spirit and flesh).*

God created each man and each woman a soul, a self, a unit, an agent, a person composed of mind (spiritual, mental, emotional, social, moral). At the same time, He created them with fleshly bodies (physical, reproductive, sexual). In the beginning man was innocent of sin and was endowed by his Creator with freedom of choice.[1] By his free choice, man sinned against God and brought sin into the human race. Salvation from sin involves the redemption of the whole man, and is offered freely to all who accept Jesus Christ as Lord and Saviour, who by shedding His own blood on the cross obtained eternal redemption for the believer. This salvation brings man back into fellowship with God and enables him to fulfill in his life, the creative purpose of God. The sacredness of human personality is evident, in that God created man in His own image and in that Christ died for man. Therefore, the idea that value resides in persons and not in animals or things, is inherent in the creative mind of God. This means that every man and woman possesses dignity, worth, and value. This sacred nature of human life should not be violated or used as a means to selfish ends. All persons are worthy of respect and Christian love.

PROPOSITION 3.

Men and women have many NEEDS *involving both soul and body.*

The purpose of life is to live according to the plan and will of God. God not only created the needs of man and woman but He created the processes through which these needs should be met. These needs and processes are morally good when they are allowed to operate according to the plan of the Creator, within the normal structure of social interaction. When man and woman live in this manner, they glorify God, their Creator.

PROPOSITION 4.

Marriage is a divinely created SOCIAL *institution.*

Not only did God create male and female but the Scriptures indicate that it was in His plan for them to associate in the social relationship we call "marriage." The nature of this social relationship is seen in Genesis 2:24, "For this cause [being created male and female] shall a man leave his father and mother and shall cleave to his wife" (see Matt. 19:5; Mark 10:7). In the traditional marriage customs in some Eastern cultures, the young man brings his bride to his home, to live with his parents, grandparents, and other relatives. On the side of the male, blood relatives live together. The weaknesses of this human system are obvious. God, through Hebrew-Christian revelation, ordained that a man should *leave* his father and mother, choose his wife and live with her in a new social unit — the man, his wife, and their children. This divinely created social unit, the family, is the cradle of human personality. It is the fountain from which human security flows, the seedbed of basic human values, the citadel of civilization, the social foundation of the Kingdom of God.

PROPOSITION 5.

Christian marriage is a PERMANENT *relationship.*

Jesus' classic statement on the duration of marriage is, "What therefore God has joined together, let not man put asunder" (Mark 10:9). The Christian concept of marriage demands a permanent one-flesh relationship between one man and one woman. This permanent relationship, called monogamy, can best meet the total needs of the husband, the wife, and their children.

It must not be assumed that the only evidence in favor of a permanent one-flesh marriage relationship is in the scriptural injunctions. There are many other pertinent facts involved. The numerical ratio of the sexes is approximately equal. During the pregnancy and nursing period of the human female, someone else must supply the needs of a woman and her offspring. The sexual desires and activities of men and women are not seasonal but are continuous. The long period of childhood from birth to adulthood involves the need for mature adults to feed, protect, and guide growing children. Growing children need love, sympathy, and understanding from their father and mother in order to develop normal personalities.

Monogamy is the simplest form of family grouping. It provides efficiency in social organization and regulation and the privacy necessary for the operation of love, sympathy, and understanding in husband-wife and parent-child relationships. All persons have a social right to know who their relatives are. Children have a right to know who their fathers are. A wife has a right to know who is the father of her children. A husband has a right to know that he is the father of his children. Only fidelity in a permanent one-flesh marriage can insure these rights. These and other similar facts, when seen together in light of the Scriptures, make it possible to say, without equivocation, that a permanent one-flesh marriage relationship *is* the creative plan of God.

PROPOSITION 6.

Marriage is a REPRODUCTIVE *relationship*.

The Scripture directs husbands and wives to "Be fruitful, and multiply, and replenish the earth" (Gen. 1:28). Scudder points out that "The creative *plan* of God is not complete until new life is born as a result of one-flesh union. . . . No normal couple should enter into marriage relations with the intent of remaining childless. To do so is to be robbed of true and complete fulfillment."[2]

PROPOSITION 7.

Marriage is a SEXUAL *relationship*.

Quoting the ancient record of Genesis (2:24), Jesus said, "They twain shall be one flesh" (Matt. 19:5). This passage refers to sexual intercourse between husband and wife in marriage. The Genesis account of creation and Jesus' interpretation of that account make it clear that "sex" originated in the mind of God. Sex is God's idea. Sexual intercourse as an act and experience is a part of God's plan for the male and female. The Hebrew-Christian teachings indicate that the "maleness" and "femaleness" of human life reflect the image of God.

PROPOSITION 8.

The sexual nature of men and women is both SPIRITUAL-EMOTIONAL-MENTAL AND PHYSICAL.

Sex, as a God-created experience, cannot be separated from spiritual-emotional-mental attitudes and feelings, An attitude of love, romance, and happiness between husband and wife promotes sexual expression. An

attitude of fear, frustration, shame, guilt, or unhappiness
blocks sexual expression. Fear is a major enemy of
normal sex life. J. A. Fritze says, "Sex is a mental
attitude. There is little if any organic motivation for a
sexual cohabitation between male and female. Organi-
cally the body compensates for its own release needs."[3]
Sylvanus M. Duvall expresses this idea in beautiful
language. "Sexual intercourse is one way in which many
feelings are channeled. . . . These feelings or emotions
may be likened to streams of water striving to find outlets. Some of them are small and feeble . . . [others are]
larger and stronger. . . . But strong or weak, great or
small, all seek to probe for channels through which they
can flow and find expression."[4]

Our society calls the spiritual-emotional-mental attitudes and feelings between sweethearts, and husbands
and wives by the beautiful word "love." Although the
attitude and feeling called love is difficult to isolate,
describe, or define, objectively we may assume that it
does exist. Love is real. It may be responded to. We can
know it. It affects us when we have it or fail to have it.
Love is not a metaphysical entity; it is a mental attitude.
It is not just infatuation; it is a relationship with sub-
stance. It is not just romance but it induces and promotes
romance in its true meaning. It is not just an instinctive
desire for reproduction. Yet it would tend to lead to
reproduction. It is certainly not just sex desire. Yet it will
move in the direction of expressing itself in sexual relationships with the person loved. It is not just a mental
fact or emotion. Yet it operates in the mental and emotional nature of persons. It is not just human relationships but it is a special kind of human relationship. It is
not just togetherness, but it fosters togetherness. It is not
just sympathy but it cares for the person involved. It is

not just empathy, but it practices empathy. It is not devotion to an ideal. It involves ideals but they are always related to persons. Love is an intimate personal attitude and emotional concern and relationship between two persons of opposite sex which is characterized by reciprocal devotion, self-sacrifice, and efforts to develop and enrich the total personality of the other. The fact that love may vary, approach perfection, wax and wane, or fail, does not change the fact that love is real. The Lutheran Family Life Committee distinguishes between love and sex by saying that "Sex serves as a medium through which love is expressed. The meeting of two bodies cannot of itself make love. It can only express a love that already exists."[5]

The importance of these spiritual-emotional-mental attitudes and feelings in sexual expression can hardly be overestimated. This aspect of sexuality represents at least 51 percent of the whole experience.

At the same time, a sexual experience is physical. Sexual expression in intercourse involves definite physical activity. This activity includes some direct physical stimulation, a union of the genital organs, a muscular tenseness, followed by a muscular explosion through the pelvic regions, spreading out over the rest of the body. This physical transaction gives physical release. The physical side of human sexuality is real, tangibly real. C. W. Scudder comments, " 'One flesh' certainly refers to a fleshly bodily union . . . Jesus used 'sarx' in Matthew 19:5 to mean 'the body.' In marriage, according to this rendering, husband and wife become 'one body.' "[6] Although the Hebrew-Christian writings did not hesitate to talk in terms of the "body," they did not separate the expression of the flesh from the total person.

The Christian concept of mind-body interaction in

sexuality is illustrated in Paul's statement, "Do you not know that your body is a temple of the Holy Spirit within you, which you have from God? You are not your own: you were bought with a price. So glorify God in your body" (1 Cor. 6:19-20, RSV). Paul was warning the Corinthian Christians against the sexual excesses prevalent in Corinth. He was saying that the human body is a "temple," a kind of "Holy of Holies" in which God's Holy Spirit resides. We are exhorted to "glorify God" in our bodies. Here we have the Hebrew-Christian thought calling for the use of the physical body in human experience in ways that are pleasing to God.

The Christian teaching on sexuality can be understood only in terms of Proposition 2, "God created man and woman as *mind-body* units." "You cannot isolate the physical from the spiritual. They belong together. The one sustains and fortifies the other. The spiritual redeems and enables the physical; the physical expresses and communicates the spiritual."[7] Any effort to ignore, avoid, block, or destroy the activity of either the spiritual-emotional-mental or the fleshly-bodily-physical nature of men and women is unchristian and unrealistic. "The body apart from the spirit is dead" (James 2:26, RSV). This is why both the materialistic and the ascetic interpretation of marriage would destroy society if either of their assumptions were allowed to control human life.

PROPOSITION 9.

Sexuality is only ONE ASPECT OF TOTAL PERSONALITY.

The physical body is a unit, but it is made up of many parts. God, in the creative plan of nature, has given significant functions to each part of the body. The different parts work together as a whole in sympathetic relationship to each other.[8] In a similar manner, the

human personality is made up of many parts or components. The sexual aspect of human nature is only one
component of total personality. Normal personality
growth involves the cooperation of all components, each
functioning according to its purpose. Sexual expression
in both man and woman involves the total person, the
total personality. J. A. Fritze remarks that "To divide the
total entity of an individual into personality and/or sex is
like trying to divide society from economics."[9]

PROPOSITION 10.

Sexuality was designed by the Creator to be a PER-
SONAL PLEASURE *relationship between husband and
wife.*

In Proverbs 5:19, a young man is instructed "to be
intoxicated continually with the delight and ecstasy of
his wife's sexual love." Sylvanus M. Duvall says, "Sexual intercourse is obviously the most intense physical
pleasure known to man. This pleasure is closely associated with the release of physical tension."[10] The Lutheran
Family Life Committee writes, "Approval of sexual pleasure . . . is implied . . . in the fact that the sheer delight of
sex is the obviously dominant theme of the Song of
Solomon." This committee summarized the Hebrew concept of sex, as follows: "Sex in the Old Testament is
clearly regarded as a valuable gift from God, not only for
the purpose of bringing children into the world but also
for the satisfaction of one of mankind's deepest needs
and for sheer enjoyment. . . . Marriage is viewed as a
divinely ordained way by which men and women satisfy
physical and emotional needs and provide for the con-
tinuation of society. Sex need not be explained or jus-
tified or covered with a halo of spirituality. Sex is good in
itself."[11]

In the past, many groups within the historical stream of Christianity have tended to shy away from the idea that God approves sex for "pleasure" between husband and wife. Most of us feel that this attitude does not rest upon Biblical concepts but rather upon the unconscious assumption of various degrees of ascetic dualism. The mind-body unity of the total person, as described above, leaves the way open for approval of sex relations between husband and wife as a "personal pleasure." God has willed to use the creation of the physical as a vehicle to promote His creative purposes. To shy away from the fact that the creative plan of God includes personal pleasure in sexual relations between husband and wife is pointless.

PROPOSITION 11.

Sexuality in marriage was planned as a MEANS TO OTHER ENDS *and never as an end in itself.*

Although we may speak of sex as a personal pleasure, it does not follow that this pleasure is to be deified and worshiped. Sexual self-control is the only ultimate road to self-realization. It is only through self-control that man can use sexuality to glorify God. The value of the pleasure of sex is in its function. Its function is to accomplish specific purposes or ends, such as more efficient personality development, improvement in the social nature of the family, and an incease in the spiritual relationships between persons and God.

PROPOSITION 12.

Sexual intercourse fuses husband and wife into a COMPLETE ONE-FLESH UNIT.

The Genesis record is emphatic that husband and wife "shall be one flesh" (2:24). Jesus, in approving this Old Testament concept, says, "They twain shall be one

flesh: so then they are no more twain but one flesh" (Mark
10:8). The nature of this "one-flesh" unity is both spiritual and physical. Scudder uses two apt illustrations,
borrowed from C. S. Lewis, to describe the intent of God
in creating the "one-flesh" experience. He says,
"Woman was created to meet the needs of man, and also
in such a way that man would meet her needs. Either
without the other is incomplete. The key and lock as one
mechanism and the violin and bow as one instrument . . .
[are] illustrative of a two-in-one unity. It may well be
noted also that neither the lock nor the key can carry out
the purpose for which it was fashioned without the other.
Together they function as a complete lock. Neither the
violin nor the bow can perform its proper function without the other, but, as someone has suggested, they can
make sweet music together — together they are a complete musical instrument. So it is with man and woman;
together they can perform the function for which they
were created. Both are incomplete until they are united
and become 'completed' man."[12]

PROPOSITION 13.

*Ultimately, the basic purpose of sexual pleasure in
marriage is to* BIND HUSBAND AND WIFE TOGETHER IN A
LIFELONG RELATIONSHIP.

If sexuality for pleasure were an end in itself, as
materialism advocates, then extra-marital sex relations
would logically follow. This point of view must be rejected. Since, in the creative plan, the pleasure of sex is
for the purpose of binding husband and wife together in a
lifelong relationship, it follows that extra-marital sex
relations are a violation of God's intentions. The evidence in the Scriptures indicates that God's intention in
creation, was for husband and wife to enjoy regular

sexual experiences throughout their lives for the purpose
of binding them together in a permanent lifelong relationship.

PROPOSITION 14.

*The unitive plan of God calls for sexual pleasure to
be a* MUTUAL *experience between husband and wife.*

This means that both husband and wife should have
a definite sexual climax, or orgasm, in their regular sexual
experiences. Fritze points out that "Normally male and
female are equally motivated mentally and emotionally
toward sexual cohabitation. The popular notion that
women are colder than men . . . is false."[13] David Mace
says that "The unitive function of sex is to consummate
the unity of the husband and wife when their marriage
begins, and continuously to renew and sustain that unity
as they go on through life together. It will achieve this
end only if it is a mutually satisfying experience. Where
one partner is seeking to take only and not to give, to
achieve individual gratification rather than to bestow
happiness, the result may be resentment and not con-
tentment. . . . What this means is that the husband and
wife must together learn the art of mutually satisfying
intercourse. This will require time and patience."[14]
(Chapters 4 and 5 describe detailed procedures to help
husband and wife make sexual expression a fully mutual
experience.)

PROPOSITION 15.

*A happy love relationship between husband and wife
provides the* PROPER HOME ENVIRONMENT *for growing,
maturing children.*

Central in the total plan of creation is the propagation of the human race (Proposition 6). According to the
creative plan, there is a long period from birth to adult

maturity. The basic needs of growing children are not sexual. They are emotional. There is much stress and strain in the long process of growing up. The bent of a child's personality development is determined by the quality of the overall parent-child relationships. The only adequate environment for growing children is a home where a happy husband and wife are deeply committed to each other and deeply love each other.

Thus, in the infinite wisdom of God, He willfully planned human life so that husband and wife could regularly express their love and commitment to each other through satisfying sexual experiences. These are designed to support, cultivate, nourish, fortify, and keep fresh personal love and devotion between husband and wife. Reproductivity and sexuality are Siamese twins in creative planning. They are two individual systems in the creative plan, yet they are complexly interrelated.

Christian leaders have not capitalized on the fact that materialistic marriage theories utterly fail at the point of providing an adequate environment for growing children.

Proposition 16.

The sacred and personal nature of sex demands MODESTY *in social relationships and* PRIVACY *in sexual relationships.*

Sexual intercourse is not just a shallow, flippant, casual episode. Rather, it is a deep core activity of the innermost being of men and women. The sexual relationship is so central and significant in human relationships that it calls for fidelity, honor, respect, self-control, and responsibility. Modesty is necessary because sex is sacred and personal. Modesty is a part of the order of divine creation. It flows from the plan, purpose, and will of God for marriage. Modesty is not to be confused with ignorance, arrogance, or a feeling of superiority. On the contrary, it is intelligence, humility, devotion, and righteousness fused into one. A modest woman can, with dignity, be gay, jolly, and jubilant. There is no evidence in our research which indicates that dignified modesty is a barrier to good sex life.

To insist on privacy in love and sexual relationships does not mean that these are evil, that we are ashamed of them, or that we have guilt feelings about them. Rather, it means that they are intimate, personal, and sacred. Love demands privacy. Love loses something when it has an audience. David Mace expresses this idea when he writes, "The best, the most stable, the most satisfying kind of marriage is that in which the couple think of their intimate life together as a secluded walled garden where no one else ever comes — a private little kingdom, apart from the rush and roar of the world's life, in which they can enjoy the full and free expression of their mutual love and be refreshed and renewed. To allow an interloper to break into that garden, or a usurper to invade that kingdom, would be to threaten the very heart of the marriage with grave danger and even with destruction."[15]

PROPOSITION 17.

There is no conflict between the process of LIVING A DEVOUT CHRISTIAN LIFE *and the process of* ACHIEVING AND ENJOYING GOOD SEXUAL ADJUSTMENT *in marriage*.

A devout Christian life and good sexual adjustment in marriage supplement each other. If a married couple is devoted to Christian ideals, this should promote efficient and happy sex life. On the other hand, good sexual adjustment in marriage should encourage a close, warm, personal spiritual relationship between a couple and God. "Christian husbands and wives, as they come together in the deeply satisfying experience which fulfills their nature and the purposes for which it was ordained, should be able to echo the Creator's joy and satisfaction and reverently to give thanks for the blessings of sexual union."[16]

PROPOSITION 18.

Sex DESTROYS *when it operates outside of the creative plan of marriage*.

"If a tree is healthy, the rain and sunshine will make it grow. If it is not healthy, those same elements will cause it to rot."[17] In a similar manner, sexual relations practiced within the creative plan make married life rich and complete. When sex is isolated and allowed to operate outside the creative plan, it is unsocial and immoral. It is sinful. Sin is an inward condition of the heart that causes people in thought, word, or deed to rebel against God, His will, and His creative plan. Sexual promiscuity paralyzes spiritual development. It erodes personal character. It disintegrates personality. It retards social responsibility. It breeds boredom, unhappiness, and despair. It destroys. Scudder feels that "All sex expressions outside of wedlock produce bitter fruit. . . ."[18] Bowman thinks that "Out of sex, rightly used, arise some of the most profound satisfactions, most meaningful human relationships, richest beauty of which man is capable. Out of sex misused arise some of the profoundest disappointments, most tragic interpersonal relationships, grossest ugliness known to man."[19]

PROPOSITION 19.

The RIGHTNESS *of sexual behavior must be determined by the creative plan of God and not by current cultural practices*.

Culture is constantly drifting, shifting, changing. The person of God, the nature of God, the creative plan of God does not change. The stream of life changes very little, if at all. The nature and needs of man and woman remain constant. The processes of reproduction and the needs of growing children follow uniform fixed patterns. It is easy to be caught in the trap of exalting superficial and insignificant social change and to ignore the near permanent nature of the creative plan of God. For the Christian community to disregard cultural drifts is unthinkable. Some adjustments to social change are always necessary. However, it is doubly unthinkable for us to cut loose from divine anchors and drift in the shallow waters of cultural change directed largely by greedy power seekers, selfish vested interests, and phony social climbers. The Christian family must stay anchored to the creative plan of God. This plan is not only known and understood through humble respect for divine revelation, but also through the objective facts of science, logical and intelligent reason, and through historical, social, and personal experience.

PROPOSITION 20.

The centrality of sex in human life calls for thorough PRE-MARRIAGE TRAINING AND COUNSELING.

Boys and girls growing up into adulthood and entering marriage do not know how to have effective sexual relationships by instinct alone. In fact, an effective sexual relationship in marriage is a rather complex process that has to be learned.

Normally, when a person moves into a new relationship or activity in our society, he is given information and instruction on how to be effective in the new experience. We do not expect children to become efficient pianists or violinists without thorough instruction. In the past, instead of giving young couples careful instruction on the process of adjusting sexually in marriage, we have allowed them to marry with little knowledge, mixed with much myth and misinformation about sex. The results of this neglect has often been tragic and sad. Because the creative plan has made sex to be of major significance in marriage, the Christian community must shift its policy and develop a program of thorough pre-marriage training and counseling in the area of sex. Some positive suggestions for pastors and other church leaders are in Appendix III.

Notes

[1]This description of man is based on the "Baptist Faith and Message" adopted by the Southern Baptist Convention in Kansas City, Missouri, May 9, 1963.

[2]C. W. Scudder, *The Family in Christian Perspective* (Nashville: Broadman Press, 1962), p. 32.

[3]An unpublished paper read before the Groves Conference on Marriage and the Family at Columbus, Ohio, April 6, 1960.

[4]Sylvanus M. Duvall, *Men, Women and Morals* (New York: Association Press, 1952), pp. 89-90.

[5]Oscar E. Feucht (Editor), *Sex and the Church* (St. Louis: Concordia Publishing House, 1961), Volume V of the Marriage and Family Research Series, p. 224.

[6]Scudder, op. cit., p. 24.

[7]David R. Mace, *Whom God Hath Joined* (Philadelphia: The Westminster Press, 1953), p. 30.

[8]See 1 Corinthians 12:14, 24-25.

[9]Fritze, op. cit., p. 1.

[10]Duvall, op. cit., p. 67.

[11]Feucht, op. cit., pp. 17, 25.

[12]Scudder, op. cit., pp. 31-32.

[13]Fritze, op. cit., p. 1.

[14]Mace, op. cit., p. 44.

[15]Mace, op. cit., p. 30.

[16]Mace, op. cit., p. 40.

[17]Clyde T. Francisco, *The Young People's Teacher* (Nashville: Convention Press, July, 1964), p. 49.

[18]Scudder, op. cit., p. 35.

[19]Henry A. Bowman, *A Christian Interpretation of Marriage* (Philadelphia: The Westminster Press, 1952), p. 15.

CHAPTER 3

Reproductive and Sexual Organs

Have you not read, that he which made them at the beginning made them male and female?
Matthew 19:4

Now the body is not one member but many . . . God has harmonised the whole body by giving importance of function to the parts . . . that the body should work together as a whole with all the members in sympathetic relationship with one another. 1 Corinthians 12:14, 24-25 (PHILLIPS)

YOUNG COUPLES entering marriage are rightly concerned about good sexual adjustment. It is not only important that they understand the Christian point of view on sexuality as described in Chapter 2, but it is also necessary that they understand the nature and purpose of the human reproductive and sexual organs. This knowl-edge should help both the husband and wife to understand themselves and each other as they enter the marriage relationship.

This chapter will present a brief sketch of both the male and female reproductive and sexual organs. The discussion should be understood in light of the Christian doctrine of sexuality. If this part of human life is rightly understood, it should increase our faith in God. There are many sources of evidence pointing to the existence of God. One of the more important of these evidences is the wonderful, intricate, complex structure of the human body. This is equally true of the reproductive and sexual systems, each of which are parts of the total unit, the body. Again and again, as we study the plan and purpose of these systems, there is abundant evidence of purposive planning by God, our Creator.

We now turn our attention to a description of the male and female reproductive and sexual organs.

MALE REPRODUCTIVE AND SEXUAL ORGANS
(See Figure 1)

GONADS. The two gonads, sometimes called *sex glands, testes,* or *testicles,* are oval-shaped organs and may be called the "factory" which produces *spermatozoa.* Spermatozoa means "living thing." Usually, in popular language, the spermatozoa are called "sperm" cells. Sperms are the male reproductive cells that unite with the female reproductive cells in order for human life to be reproduced. Also, the gonads produce a male sex hormone called *testosterone* which plays a vital part in producing male body characteristics such as body shape, voice, hair, etc. The process of reproducing sperm cells begins at approximately age 13 to 14. This period in a boy's life is called puberty. The production of these cells continues in healthy males past middle age, and often on into old age. The gonads are enclosed in the *scrotum* which is a fleshy sac suspended between the thighs and united to the body torso.

EPIDIDYMIS. The Greek "epi" means "upon" and "didymis" means "gonad." Thus, the *epididymis* is that which is upon the gonad. It is a coiled tube attached to the top of the gonad. The sperm cells move out of the gonad into the epididymis where they remain for a time, while they mature. The epididymis is often called a temporary storage vessel for the sperm cells.

VAS DEFERENS. The Latin "vas" means "vessel" and "deferens" means "to carry." Thus, the *vas deferens* is a "vessel for carrying something." It is a long tube connected with the epididymis. It extends beyond the scrotum into the body cavity through a small opening of muscles in the abdominal wall. Inside the body cavity, the vas deferens eventually empties into the *urethra*, the tube inside the penis that also drains the bladder.

SEMINAL VESICLES. The word "seminal" means "semen." *Semen* is made up of sperm cells and a fluid that carries the sperms. The word "vesicle" means "vessel" or "sac." Although the seminal vesicles appear to serve as a second temporary storage reservoir, they share this responsibility with the *ampulla*. The ampulla is the enlarged upper end of the vas deferens. The seminal vesicles also secrete fluid which becomes a part of the semen.

PROSTATE GLAND. The *prostate gland* is muscular and glandular. It provides a secretion that becomes a part of the semen. The muscular part of the prostate glands, together with the seminal vesicles and the rigid penis, contracts and ejaculates (discharges) the semen through the urethra and to the outside of the body.

PENIS. The *penis* is both an internal and an exter-

nal organ. It is composed of porous tissues which are a
honeycombed network of blood vessels. Under sexual
stimulation, blood rushes into these blood vessels. At the
same time, small valves are automatically closed, pre-
venting the blood from flowing out. As stimulation continues, blood flows in, the penis fills up, tightens, and
stands rigid and erect. When stimulation ceases, or an
ejaculation takes place, the small valves gradually open
and the excess blood flows back into the circulatory
system. This process of the ejaculation of the semen is
called *orgasm*. Popular language often uses the term
"climax." This system of erection of the penis and ejaculation of the semen, for the purpose of depositing it in the
vagina of the female to bring about conception, is a major
and skillful engineering accomplishment on the part of
the divine Creator.

When the penis is in the relaxed state, it is about
3½ to 4 inches in length. In its state of erection, it is
about 5 to 6½ inches in length.

The head of the penis is called *glans penis* and is a
little larger than the shaft of the penis. The glans penis
contains a heavy concentration of nerve endings which
play a major role in the sexual arousal of the male. These
nerve endings are no different than those in other parts of
the body except they are more densely concentrated in
the glans penis. Usually, at birth, the glans penis is
encircled with a thick layer of skin called *prepuce* or
foreskin. It is important that the opening in the foreskin of
the adult male be large enough to allow the head of the
erect penis to move back and forth without pain or
excess tightness. When this condition does not prevail,
the person needs to be circumcised. Circumcision is
a simple operation in which a surgeon cuts the top of the
foreskin away, thus freeing the glans penis from its

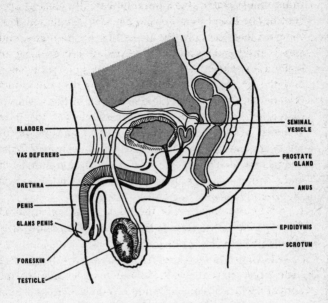

Figure One. Male Reproductive Organs

covering. The purpose of circumcision is twofold, (1) to permit effective sanitation, and (2) to permit normal sexual experiences and sexual control. Although the Jews used circumcision as a religious symbol, there is evidence that they possessed insight concerning its practicality. (At the birth of a male child, couples should instruct the attending physician to perform circumcision, if it is needed.)

FEMALE REPRODUCTIVE AND SEXUAL ORGANS
(See Figures 2 and 3)

LABIA MAJORA. The Latin "labia" means "lips" and "majora" means "major or large." The *labia majora* are large lips, composed of thick round fleshy folds of tissue, covered with hair. They protect the genital organs beneath, which are covered with tender mucous membrane.

LABIA MINORA, The Latin "labia minora" means "small lips." They are located inside the large outer lips. They are small thin folds of tissue covered with mucous membrane.

CLITORIS. The word "clitoris" is derived from the Greek word *kleitoris* meaning "to shut up." This has reference to the organ being concealed by the outer and inner lips. The *clitoris* in the female corresponds to the penis in the male. It is located at the outer uppermost point where the inner lips meet. It is similar to the penis in two ways. (1) It is composed of a shaft, glans (head), and prepuce (foreskin). The foreskin is a small hood that partially covers the clitoris. It is made up of the inner lips at the point where they join together. (2) The glans of the clitoris is composed of a dense concentration of nerve endings, designed to produce sexual arousal when under stimulation. The clitoris is different from the penis in that

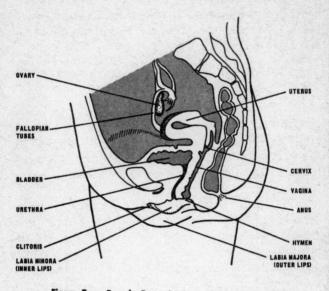

Figure Two. Female Reproductive and Sexual Organs

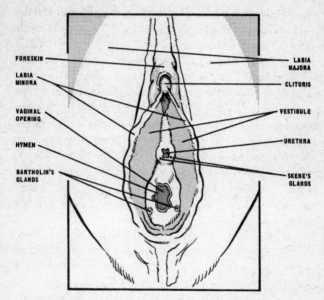

Figure Three. Vulva or External Female Organs

(1) it has no opening, (2) it ejaculates nothing, and (3) it does not directly play a part in the process of reproduction. It is exclusively an organ of sexual sensation. It is the external trigger that sets off sexual arousal and orgasm.

The labia majora, labia minora, the clitoris, and the outer opening of the vagina make up the external female organs. They are often called the "vulva" or "genitals."

VAGINA. The word "vagina" is a Latin word meaning "scabbard," that is, a sheath that encloses a sword or bayonet, to shield and protect it. The *vagina* is the passage between the vulva and the womb that receives the male penis in sexual intercourse. It is composed of delicate muscle tissue lined with mucous membrane which lies in loosely flowing folds. Normally it is approximately 3½ inches in length but can stretch to six or more inches in length without discomfort. It is also a reproductive organ, in that it is the passageway for the menstrual flow, and is the birth canal.

HYMEN. The word "hymen" is a Greek word meaning "skin" or "membrane." The hymen is a fold of mucous membrane partly enclosing the opening of the vagina, lying at the back part of the opening. It generally tends to block sexual intercourse. It varies in size, structure and thickness. Some hymens are so thin and plastic that they survive sexual intercourse without being broken. In a few (very few) cases the hymen is entirely absent. In some cases the hymen may possibly be broken by some excessive physical activity or by a physical accident. In other cases, it may be necessary for a physician to break the hymen for medical purposes. On the other hand some hymens are so thick and strong that it is impossible to break them in sexual intercourse. When this is the case, it is necessary to have a physician stretch or cut them. This may be determined at the time of the pre-marital pelvic examination. When a hymen is broken in first intercourse, there may be slight or considerable pain, and some bleeding. The amount of pain and bleeding would be determined by the structure and thickness of the hymen.

UTERUS. The word "uterus" is a Latin word usually translated "womb." The *uterus* or *womb* is a pear-shaped muscular organ about 3½ inches long and 2 inches wide. It is the home in which the human embryo is protected and developed before birth. The smaller end of the uterus opens into the upper portion of the vagina and is known as the "cervix." The opening between the uterus and the vagina is called the mouth of the cervix. The muscular strength of the walls of the uterus is the major force which expels the baby through the vaginal passage at birth.

OVARY. The word "ovary" is a form of the Latin word "ovum" which means "egg." The two female *ovaries*, one on each side of the body cavity, correspond to the male gonads. Besides producing hormones, which determine the female body characteristics, the ovaries produce reproductive cells called "ova." In popular language the ova ("ovum" is the singular) are usually called "egg" cells.

There are about 300,000 to 400,000 egg cells in the ovaries of a normal baby girl. Only about 450 of these mature and are sent out to the uterus, one each month, from puberty to menopause.

FALLOPIAN TUBES. The word "fallopian" is the name of an Italian anatomist who did much research related to the *fallopian tubes*. These two tubes are the passageways from the ovaries to the uterus. Each tube is about four inches in length. They are not directly connected to the ovaries. The finger-like projections of the larger end of the tubes intercept the egg cell when it is released from the ovary and start it on its way to the uterus.

Young couples, ready for marriage, need to understand the basic processes involved in the nature of *conception* and of menstruation. One egg is released from an ovary each month or on the average of every 28 days. The release of the egg from the ovary is called the *ovulation* period. When sperm cells are deposited in the vagina, they travel quickly through the cervical opening into the uterus and scatter throughout the fallopian tubes. For conception to occur, sexual intercourse must take place at, or near, the time of the ovulation period. Medical science is not certain about the life span of the egg and the sperm. Some scholars suggest about 12 hours for the egg and 24 hours for the sperm. Others suggest 48-72 hours for both egg and sperm. When a live egg cell encounters a live sperm cell, the two unite and conception is accomplished. Usually, conception occurs in the fallopian tubes. The fertilized egg is moved gradually, over a period of three to five days, through the fallopian tubes into the uterus. Here it is implanted in the wall of the uterus and gradually develops for a period of approximately nine months. The period from conception to birth is called "pregnancy."

The menstrual period is a vital part of the reproductive nature of women. The word "menstrual" is derived from the Latin word "mensis" meaning "month." During the period in which the egg cell is being developed in the ovary, the lining inside the uterus increases in thickness and an extra supply of blood comes into it. The increased lining of the uterus is for the purpose of anchoring the fertilized egg and the extra supply of blood is for the

purpose of nourishing it during its development. When
no sperm cell is present to fertilize the egg, it soon dies
and the elaborate preparations that had been taking
place inside the uterus are now useless. Therefore the
increased lining of the uterus and the increased supply of
blood are expelled from the body through the vagina.
And the process starts over again. This monthly cycle
begins at approximately age 12 to 13 (puberty) and
continues until approximately age 45 to 50. The ceas-
ing of this cycle is called "*menopause*." The word
"menopause" comes from two Greek words meaning "to
cease" or "to stop."

The process of reproduction and the process of the
menstrual cycle are two more examples of major engineering achievements planned by the infinite mind of
the Creator-God.

(Attention pastors and counselors: for a fuller dis-
cussion of the nature and functions of the male and
female reproductive and sexual organs, see Dr. Ed
Wheat's cassettes *Sexual Problems and Sex Technique in
Marriage* and Masters and Johnson's *Human Sexual
Response*.)

CHAPTER 4

Basic Methods of Sexual Adjustment in Marriage

> *My son, be attentive to my wisdom, incline your ear to my understanding . . . drink water from your own cistern, flowing water from your own well. Should your springs be scattered abroad, streams of water in the streets? Let them be for yourself alone and not for strangers with you. Let your fountain be blessed, and rejoice in the wife of your youth, a lovely hind, a graceful doe. Let her affection fill you at all times with delight, be infatuated always with her love.* Proverbs 5:1, 15-19 (RSV)

WE HAVE discussed in Chapter 2 the fact that we Christians do not think sex, as such, is evil. Sex is God's idea. We accept it as such. Sex is the servant of Christianity. To a Christian, sex in marriage according to the plan of God, our Creator, is good, beautiful, and sacred. It is only the abuse and misuse of sex that is evil. We not only feel that sex, as such, is not evil, but we feel that churches, pastors, Christian leaders, and parents have a responsibility to help prepare couples for responsible sex life in marriage. The purpose of this chapter is to introduce couples planning marriage to broad principles and factual knowledge concerning basic methods in sexual adjustment in marriage.

Couples planning marriage and reading this book for the first time, either together or separately, may not find many ideas that they have not heard something about before. So they should not be expecting too much new information. Yet, in spite of considerable thought and reading, there will probably still be some questions, some anxieties, and possibly some latent fears about the sexual side of marriage. Perhaps some ideas will not be very clear. It is our hope to clear up and crystallize the reader's thinking on these points. When the prospective bride and groom read these chapters and discuss them together a few weeks before marriage, then they can move into their marriage and honeymoon with confidence that they both have the same knowledge. This fact is one of the major values of pre-marriage counseling.

THE NATURE OF SEXUAL AROUSAL

Let us begin the discussion of sexual adjustment in marriage with the illustration of a piano-violin duet. A piano and a violin are two different instruments, very different. Yet, when two musicians, playing the instruments, do the right thing, at the right time, in the right attitude, beautiful music is the result. Likewise, the physical bodies of a bride and groom are different, very different. Yet, when they in marriage as husband and wife do the right thing, at the right time, and in the right attitude, they will have beautiful sexual harmony as they express their love to each other. It is our solemn responsibility now to describe how husband and wife may do the right thing, at the right time, and in the right attitude in order to become *one flesh* in marriage. Most of the rest of this book will be concerned with these details.

There is one general rule discussed briefly in Chapter 2 that must be followed. Let us review and emphasize this important truth. Husband and wife are responsible to meet each other's sexual needs all of their married lives. The husband is responsible to meet his wife's sexual needs. He must regularly and lovingly arouse her to a complete sexual experience, climax (or orgasm). Likewise, the wife must meet her husband's sexual needs. She must regularly and lovingly arouse him to a sexual experience, climax (or orgasm). A husband should not expect his wife to meet her own sexual needs. Neither should a wife expect her husband to meet his own sexual needs. Rather, motivated by love, they will want to meet each other's sexual needs. In this manner, both of their sexual needs will be met in the most satisfying and beautiful manner.

In 1 Corinthians 7:2-5 we have these words: ". . . each man should have his own wife and each woman her own husband. The husband should give to his wife her conjugal rights and likewise the wife to her husband" (RSV). In this passage, "conjugal" means sexual. This Scripture is saying that the husband should meet his wife's sexual needs and the wife should meet her husband's sexual needs. This Scripture continues, "For the wife does not rule over her own body, but the husband does; likewise the husband does not rule over his own body, but the wife does." In marriage the wife's body does not belong to her. It belongs to her husband and he rules over it. In like manner, in marriage, the husband's body does not belong to him. It belongs to his wife, and she rules over it.

This passage is saying that in marriage each rules over each other's sexual life by meeting each other's sexual needs. In verse five, Paul says, "Do not refuse one another," that is, do not refuse to meet each other's sexual needs. This passage makes it clear that both husband and wife are morally responsible to meet each other's sexual needs.

There are two major problems that tend to block good sexual adjustment in marriage. To make it easy to remember these two problems, we will call them "time" and "space" and discuss them in order.

By "time," we refer to the fact that, sexually, male and female bodies are "timed" differently. Sexually, man is timed quickly. He can become aroused through sexual stimulation with his wife and usually reach an orgasm in a very short time, two minutes, one minute, or even in less time. This is normal for him. He will gradually learn to control himself, but he will always tend to be "quick on the trigger" until he gradually slows down during middle age and the years that follow. His wife should never say to him, "You beast, why don't you control yourself?" She should understand him in terms of his quick timing sexually, and that God created him this way. She should realize that all other women's husbands are "quick on the trigger" just like her husband is quick to respond sexually. Of course, the young husband will try to control himself as much as possible, and will learn to do so.

On the other hand, sexually, a woman is timed more slowly, sometimes very slowly, as compared with a man. We can safely say that it takes the average woman ten to fifteen minutes or longer from the time she starts sexual arousal with her husband until she experiences an orgasm. This is after she is married and is experienced in regular sexual relationships. Sometimes she may have an orgasm in ten minutes, five minutes, or even less. A few women on special occasions may have an orgasm in one or two minutes. This is the exception. At other times it may take 20 or 30 minutes, or even longer. It may vary according to where she is in the menstrual cycle. Also, other circumstances such as personal, family, or community problems may affect her. A young wife will gradually learn how to move toward her orgasm a little more quickly, but she cannot change the fact that her sexual arousal nature is timed slowly. Her husband should never say to her, "You iceberg, why don't you hurry up?" He should understand her in terms of the fact that she is not responsible for being timed slowly. He should realize that all men's wives are just like his and that God created them this way. Sex in woman is as definite, as real, and as satisfying as it is in man, but it is something deep down inside of her, a spiritual gold mine. The young husband must, with patience, love, understanding, and tenderness, uncover her sexual interest, layer by layer, and gradually bring it to the surface, allowing her to express her love for him in an orgasm. This simply takes time.

When a young couple understands their difference in sexual timing and when they accept it and cooperate with it, it is no longer a major problem, but actually may be a blessing. Let us repeat, a couple must *understand it, accept it,* and *cooperate with it* for it to be a blessing. By being a blessing, we mean that this period of sexual stimulation and arousal, whether it be 10 or 20 minutes, may become one of the sweetest, most meaningful and spiritual experiences in husband-wife relationships. It is only when a couple does not understand or does not cooperate with their differences in sexual timing that it becomes a problem.

The second major problem that tends to block good sexual adjustment we have called "space." "Space" refers to the distance on the body of the wife between the clitoris and the vaginal passage. The clitoris is the external arousal trigger that sets off the orgasm in woman. It is made up of many nerve endings designed by the Creator to arouse a woman to an orgasm. These nerve endings must be stimulated directly by physical contact for a woman to become sexually aroused high enough to have an orgasm. The clitoris is located, somewhat out in front, at the upper meeting point of the inner lips, or labia minora. Please note that on the average-sized woman the distance from the clitoris to the vaginal passage is approximately one and one-fourth inches. This is the space we are discussing.

Now, visualize the position of the vaginal passage. Note that in the process of sexual intercourse in the man-above position, the penis moves into the vagina, not from an angle above the vaginal opening, but actually from an angle slightly below it. When this fact is visualized and understood, it should be clear that in normal sexual intercourse the penis does not touch or contact the clitoris. This fact is of major importance. Since the penis does not move back and forth over the clitoris in intercourse, the wife may not become fully aroused and thus will not have an orgasm.

A couple may use other positions for intercourse in which the penis can be forced to move back and forth over the clitoris and stimulate it directly. However, there are two problems involved in doing this. First, these positions may not be very comfortable for either the wife or her husband. Secondly, many husbands cannot control themselves for ten or fifteen minutes of this type of intercourse without reaching an orgasm before their wives are fully aroused.

Since the clitoris is the arousal trigger of the wife, and since the penis does not contact the clitoris in normal intercourse, marriage counselors recommend what is called "direct" stimulation. That is, the husband, in the process of love-play before intercourse starts, will gently stimulate all the erotic zones of his wife's body. This includes kissing her lips and breasts and using his hands and fingers to explore and stimulate her total body, including the inner thighs, her labia minora, the opening of the vagina, and finally her clitoris. He will continue stimulation of the clitoris for ten or fifteen minutes, or whatever time it takes, until he is certain she is fully aroused sexually and ready for intercourse. There is nothing wrong in this procedure. Remember the piano-violin duet. A couple must do the right thing at the right time in the right attitude for full arousal and complete love harmony. It is normal in the love-play and arousal period for a couple to touch and handle each other's sexual organs. This is a pleasant and meaningful part of love expression. It was planned this way by the Creator.

This process of arousal will be discussed in detail in Chapter 5. The important point to remember here is that the *clitoris is the external arousal* trigger; that there must be uninterrupted stimulation of the clitoris and the area close to the clitoris for a wife to have an orgasm. The *method* of stimulation of the clitoris is not so important. Any one of several different methods may be satisfactory. The fact that the clitoris *has to be stimulated* is the *important thing* to remember. If a couple can give the wife sufficient stimulation simply through the process of intercourse alone to experience orgasms regularly, fine, wonderful! But few can do this during the first part of their marriage. We have simply said that direct stimulation in the arousal period is one of the surest ways for a young bride to reach an orgasm in the early part of marriage. Our research shows that 40 percent of wives, after they have gotten used to sex life in marriage, are able to become aroused and experience orgasm through intercourse only, and no manual stimulation of the clitoris is necessary. It took several weeks for most of these couples to learn how to succeed in this manner. All couples would do well to work toward this goal. However, we need to be reminded that 60 percent of all women need direct stimulation of the clitoris in the arousal process before they can reach orgasms in intercourse. Couples should not hesitate to use this method when there is need for it.

There are two types of sexual experiences that are normal for married couples to enjoy. The first type is sexual intercourse. This, of course, involves the vaginal passage and the penis. That is, after a period of love-play and sexual arousal, including direct stimulation of the clitoris, the husband and wife attempt to reach orgasms together, or one following the other by the movement of the penis back and forth in the vaginal passage. This full embrace is the most complete and meaningful sexual experience possible. Couples should *always* have this type of sexual experience *whenever possible*.

However, there will come times in marriage when couples cannot have sexual intercourse. During these times they will both have their regular and normal sexual needs. Let me discuss three examples. First, we will assume, at this point, that intercourse will not take place during the menstrual period. This period involves four to six days per month. During this time a couple would normally have intercourse one or two times, but because of the menstrual period, they would have to refrain, which they could do. Let us imagine a husband and wife who normally had intercourse every three days, but because of a special set of circumstances over which they had no control, had gone five days without intercourse. By this time they would probably be very anxious. Let us assume that they had planned intercourse on the night of the fifth day, but during the afternoon the menstrual period shows up two or three days early. Suppose the period lasts for five days. This means the couple would have to wait ten days before being able to have intercourse. Normally they would have sexual intercourse two or three times during ten days. It is true that under these circumstances a couple can refrain. However, this is not necessary.

A second example involves the time before and after a baby is born. Normally a doctor will instruct prospective parents not to have intercourse during the six weeks before a baby is born and the six weeks after it is born. The time will vary according to the condition of the prospective mother. It is well for a couple to ask the doctor for instruction about when to stop having intercourse before a baby is born, and when to start after it is born. The doctor must instruct on this matter. However, on the average, there will be a period of at least three months when it will be necessary to abstain from sexual intercourse. During this time normal sexual needs will continue. It is possible to abstain from all sexual relations during this time, but this is unrealistic and unnecessary.

A third example is when a couple wants to express their love in a sexual experience but do not have adequate contraceptives available, and feel strongly that they cannot run the risk of a pregnancy at this time. Reason would dictate that under these circumstances a couple should refrain from sexual intercourse. But it does not follow that they would avoid all sexual expression.

Marriage counselors recommend that during these and other similar times when couples cannot have intercourse, that they practice a second type of sexual experience in which they do not have intercourse and do not use the vaginal passage. This second type of sexual experience is called "sexual interstimulation." That is, husband and wife simply bring each other to orgasms through love-play and direct stimulation. The husband will stimulate the wife's clitoris with his fingers until she is aroused to experience an orgasm. At the same time, the wife will stimulate the husband's penis with her fingers until he reaches an orgasm. Through skillful love-play, stimulation, and response, the husband and wife lying in each other's arms can often have orgasms at the same time or nearly so. Let us repeat that no other type of sexual experience can take the place of sexual intercourse. However, when husband and wife cannot have intercourse for justifiable reasons, sexual interstimulation — stimulating each other to orgasms — can be as meaningful to both of them in this limited set of circumstances as having orgasms in sexual intercourse.

Let us hasten to say that there is nothing about this experience, under these circumstances, that is evil or a violation of Christian concepts. It is not a type of masturbation. This experience is not self-stimulation. It is the process of a husband and wife, who are in love with each other, stimulating each other to express their love for each other in a mutual sexual experience. This makes it possible for a couple to have a sexual experience, either by intercourse or by interstimulation, whenever they need to, all of their lives, except when they are spatially

separated from each other or one or both of them is ill.
Most doctors recommend that couples return to regular
sex relations (either sexual intercourse or interstimulation) as soon as possible after surgery or major illness.
They further recommend that normal sexual relations
between husband and wife not be interrupted during
many minor illnesses. Lack of interruption tends to reduce much strain on the marriage and promotes emotionally healthy love relationships between husband and
wife. When in doubt, couples should seek advice from
their doctor. Peter Dickinson, in his book *Fires of Au-
tumn* (Drake Publishers, Inc., 1974), has a chapter
dealing with the extent to which surgery and major and
minor illnesses should affect a couple's sexual life. We
have discussed this because some couples in marriage
hesitate to practice this second type of sexual experience, having a vague idea that it might be wrong. We are
safe in saying that all responsible Christian marriage
counselors would approve this type of experience in
marriage as being normal and good.

THE NATURE OF THE HYMEN

Often there are some problems in first sexual experiences involving the hymen. As described in Chapter
3, the hymen is a membrane located on the inside of the
opening of the vagina. Hymens vary in thickness. Sometimes a hymen is by nature so thin and elastic that it
stretches and is not broken in intercourse. The penis can
enter the vaginal passage at first intercourse with only a
feeling of tightness. In a few cases the hymen may be
entirely absent. Also, it may have been broken by a
physical accident, or by a physician for medical purposes. On the other hand, some hymens are so thick and
tough that it is impossible for the couple to have inter-

course. That is, the hymen so closes the opening of the vaginal passage that it is impossible for the penis to enter the opening. In our research we found that slightly over 13 percent of the brides in the sample had to have a doctor either stretch or cut the hymen before they could have intercourse. So we may say that approximately 87 percent of hymens may be broken in intercourse and that 13 percent can be broken only with difficulty if at all.

There are two other factors involved in the success of entrance at first intercourse on the wedding night. One is the fact that the girl has a set of muscles around the opening of the vaginal passage. Tenseness at the time of first intercourse may cause these muscles to contract and partially close the vagina. A second factor involved is the size of the groom's penis. The size of the penis varies just as people vary in height and build. One cannot judge the size of the penis by the size of the man. There may be a large man with a small penis, or a small man with a large penis. There is no basis for a man with a large penis to feel proud or superior, or for a man with a smaller penis to feel inferior or humiliated. The fact is that the size of the penis has little to do with good sex life.

But with regard to the problem of first entrance; it is obvious that, if on the wedding night the bride has a thick hymen plus some nervous tenseness, and the groom has a rather large penis, the couple could expect some problems in first intercourse. For these reasons, marriage counselors recommend that the prospective bride go to a doctor at least two to four weeks before her wedding date and request a pelvic examination, which includes the hymen, the vagina, and the womb. If she has a thick, tight hymen the doctor will detect it and recommend that it be stretched or cut. Only a doctor is qualified to do this. If the prospective bride plans to use an oral contraceptive, she should see her doctor six to eight weeks before the wedding date.

To throw further light on this idea, let us describe the experiences of some couples in our research sample. In the first case, the bride-to-be following the advice of her pre-marriage counseling went to a doctor two weeks before her wedding date and requested a pelvic examination. The doctor was busy, and for some reason he did not want to give her the examination. He said, "You'll be all right without one." Taking his advice, she was married without the examination. On their seven-day honeymoon she and her husband found that they could not have intercourse. Try as they would, they could not get the penis into the vaginal passage. On their honeymoon they became well acquainted with each other, enjoyed orgasms by interstimulation, and, in general, had a wonderful experience except that they did not have intercourse. When they came back from the honeymoon, the young wife went to another doctor and explained her problem. When he examined her, he found that she had an extremely thick, tough hymen. It was necessary for her to go to a hospital where the doctor cut the hymen, and she was in the hospital four days. This couple was married one month when they had intercourse for the first time.

Another couple had a similar experience. The modest young bride refused to go to a doctor for a pelvic examination, although her sweetheart really wanted her to do so. He rightly allowed her to make the decision. On the honeymoon, they attempted intercourse five different times and each time could not get the penis into the vaginal passage. Each time they failed, she cried. But her husband was patient, gentle, and kind to her. In each attempt she learned to relax a little more. On the sixth attempt, after careful and determined persistence, they managed to force the penis into the vagina for the first time. In spite of considerable pain and some bleeding, she did not cry, but was exceedingly happy, as she was determined not to go to a doctor. Marriage counselors feel that it would have been far wiser for this young bride to have gone to a doctor prior to her marriage.

These illustrations are given to prepare young couples just in case they should have similar complications. When there is a thick hymen, there is nothing for the bride to be embarrassed about. This is simply nature. Once a thick hymen is out of the way, sex life can be fully normal.

When the hymen is broken in first intercourse, there may be some pain and some bleeding. The amount of the pain and bleeding would be determined by the thickness of the hymen. Generally the pain and/or bleeding is not major and is often almost negligible. In some cases, pain may continue for several attempts at intercourse. With a little experience and better relaxation, the pain will gradually disappear. Our research reveals that first intercourse was slightly painful for 52 percent of the brides and considerably painful for 28 percent. For 63 couples it took from 3 to 9 experiences of sexual intercourse before the pain ceased. It took 17 couples from 19 to 25 experiences before the pain ceased. When the facts are all considered, marriage counselors almost unanimously recommend a pre-marriage pelvic examination. It is best for a girl to go to her personal family physician. The cost of the examination is generally the same as that of a regular office call.

The doctor will protect his patient as much as possible. A nurse will assist him during the examination.

Certainly it is better psychology for a bride to go into her marriage after a doctor has assured her that she should have few or no complications. If the doctor finds a hymen that would obstruct sexual intercourse, the couple should request him to stretch or cut it before the marriage. It is understood that the groom-to-be would be informed about this and would approve it. Any young husband-to-be who insists that it is his prerogative to break the hymen on the wedding night and refuses to allow his bride to have a pelvic examination is displaying both his selfishness and his ignorance. Possible pain and bleeding are not contributing factors to a pleasant honeymoon. Since one has only one honeymoon, it is better to be able to remember it as a pleasant experience.

SOME GENERAL QUESTIONS DISCUSSED

There are several general questions concerning sexual adjustment in marriage that most young couples would like to have discussed. We will now discuss seven of them.

First question, "How many orgasms are normal for husband and wife in one sexual experience?" For young married couples, one orgasm is usually sufficient for one sexual experience. When a man has one orgasm, he cannot have another until some time has passed. This is natural for all men. Generally, for young women, one orgasm is sufficient. However, some women need multiple orgasms — two, three, or more — to give them a full sexual release. This need may increase after a few months or years of marriage. When a wife cannot relax and seems to be rather nervous after one orgasm, this may be an indication that she has only had a partial sexual release. Our research indicates that for 79 percent of wives one orgasm is sufficient to meet their needs, while 18 percent say that more than one orgasm is needed sometimes, and only 3 percent seem to need more than one orgasm most of the time. If a couple plans multiple orgasms for the wife, stimulation for the next orgasm should begin not later than a few short seconds after the completion of the previous orgasm.

A second question, "How often should couples have sex relations?" The best answer is, as often as they want to, can, and have the opportunity. During the first weeks of married life, couples have relations more often. This is normal. However, after the first few weeks, intercourse about every three days or twice per week is generally sufficient. A few have relations every two days, and some every four to five days, according to their needs. If a husband and wife have been separated from each other a week or two, when they get back together, they may have intercourse twice in one day or three days in a row.

Our research shows members of our sample having a sexual experience (intercourse or interstimulation) on the average of every 3.3 days. Three percent have a sexual experience every day, 30 percent every two days, 34 percent every three days, 21 percent every four days, and 12 percent every five days or longer. When asked how often they would like to have intercourse and orgasms if they could have this experience every time they wanted to, the husbands' replies averaged every 2.7 days and the wives' replies averaged every 3.2 days. Thirty-nine percent of husbands wanted this experience more often than their wives, while 8 percent of wives wanted this experience more often than their husbands. In 53 percent of the cases, both husband and wife had the same needs. This means that 61 percent of wives wanted a sexual experience as often or more often than their husbands. These findings indicate that the traditional concept that women are not really interest in sex life is not in accord with reality.

During the first twenty or twenty-five years of married life, the husband will probably want intercourse more often than the wife. During the last twenty or twenty-five years, the wife will probably want intercourse more often than the husband. Both husband and wife should adjust themselves to meet each other's sexual drive and needs. When both are motivated by love and Christian principles, this seldom presents a major problem. Restraint and intelligent control is always better than excessive indulgence. It is well to avoid routine, such as having relations only on Tuesdays and Fridays. Often the regular course of daily life forces routine into love life, and a couple simply have to plan the experience. Couples should avoid sameness and routine, if possible. Love and sex expression thrives on spontaneous experiences. Let us repeat, in marriage it is normal for husband and wife to have intercourse whenever they both want to, can, and have the opportunity.

A third question, "Who should bring up the matter of having sex relations, the husband or the wife?" The answer is, both of them should bring it up. Many times the experience will be spontaneous and, thus, they both will bring it up together. This is excellent. Our research shows that in the first part of married life 68 percent of sexual experiences are spontaneous and only 32 percent are pre-planned. But as life moves on, many times circumstances will be such that experiences will have to be planned and either the husband or wife will have to bring it up. In marriage, if either would like to have a sexual experience, they should simply tell the other one. They should not hesitate. They should not stand back and wait for the other one to bring it up. When both husband and wife face frankly their sexual needs and turn to each other for satisfaction, this is excellent marriage adjustment.

A fourth question, "What about experimenting with different positions in sexual relations?" We recommend that couples feel free to experiment with other positions in intercourse. Some experimentation in the love-play period adds variety to love life. Although most couples use the "man-above" position most of the time, they enjoy other positions some of the time. A few couples adopt other positions regularly because it seems to meet their particular needs.

Our research indicates that 91 percent of couples use the man-above position all of the time or most all of the time. Fifty-four percent of couples experiment frequently with other positions, but usually finish with the man-above position. Only 4 percent use some position other than the man-above position more than half of the time, and only 5 percent use some other position all of the time.

It is important to the husband to have his feet firmly against the foot of the bed or some solid object to aid him in giving full expression to his sexual orgasm. In case of a bed that has no footboard, the couple may reverse their position so that his feet rest against the headboard.

The wife-above position allows the husband to relax and control himself, and permits the wife to initiate the movement necessary to give her the most stimulation by forcing the clitoris to move over the penis. The disadvantages are that this position is often not comfortable for the wife, the husband may have difficulty in controlling his arousal, and neither are in proper position to give fullest expression during orgasms. For some couples the advantages outweigh the disadvantages. This position is often advantageous for a large husband and a small wife.

Another useful position is for both husband and wife to lie on their sides facing the same direction with the husband back of the wife. The penis is moved into the vaginal passage from the rear. The disadvantages are that the penis cannot contact the clitoris and the couple cannot kiss during the experience. The advantages are that the position is very comfortable, the husband can easily use his fingers to stimulate his wife's clitoris, and he can control his own arousal. There are other slight variations of this approach. Many couples use this position for the arousal period and shift quickly to the man-above position for orgasms.

In interpersonal relationships in the community and society, modesty is a queen among virtues, but in the privacy of the marriage bedroom, behind locked doors, and in the presence of pure married love, there is no such thing as modesty. *A couple should feel free to do whatever they both enjoy which moves them into a full expression of their mutual love in a sexual experience.*

At this point it is well to give a word of caution. *All sex experiences should be those which both husband and wife want. Neither, at any time, should force the other to do anything that he does not want to do. Love does not force.*

A fifth question, "What is the best procedure for the love-play and arousal period?" There is no one set standard or procedure that should be followed. Actually, there are many possible procedures. In general, the love-play period begins with spontaneous, endearing conversation, with love pats, with hugs, and with kisses. Gradually, couples undress each other. The husband may caress and kiss his wife's body, her lips, her breasts.

Finally he will caress her sexual organs. In this process, the husband will want to stimulate his wife in the manner she enjoys and loves the most. A couple should be extremely frank with each other about what they enjoy and what produces sexual arousal.

After the period of relaxed love-play, it is generally efficient for the wife to lie down in the center of the bed on her back, pull her feet up to her hips, open her knees wide, and place her feet flat on the mattress. This puts her in a comfortable and relaxed position. Her husband should lie down on her right side placing his left arm under her neck. In this position he can hug her, kiss her neck, lips, and breasts, and at the same time, his right hand is free to reach down and stimulate her clitoris. Her hands are free to fondle his penis. Or she can place her hand on his hand and direct his stimulation of her clitoris. This position of sexual arousal is described in the Bible in the Song of Solomon 2:6 and 8:3. These two verses are identical. They read as follows: "Let his left hand be under my head and his right hand embrace me." The word "embrace" could be translated "fondle" or "stimulate." Here in the Bible, in a book dealing with pure married love, a married woman expresses herself with longing that her husband put his left arm under her head and that he uses his right hand to stimulate her clitoris.

This position of sexual arousal seems to have been the position used by many people back through the centuries. We do not hesitate to say that the general arousal procedure described here is a part of the plan of God as He created man and woman. Therefore, mankind has used this procedure because it is the plan of God and because it is efficient.

During the arousal period, it is an extra stimulus for

the wife to fondle the husband's penis. This adds to the mutuality and fullness of the arousal method as described above. However, often this is too much stimulation for the husband. Self-control is necessary at this point for him. Only experience can determine whether or not a couple can use this part of the procedure.

In this whole arousal process the couple should take their time and concentrate on the arousal of the wife. She should turn herself loose and the husband should control himself. This process should continue until the wife is aroused near an orgasm and ready for intercourse.

A sixth question, "What about sex relations during the menstrual period?" We recommend that couples do not have sexual intercourse during the menstrual period at the beginning of their married life, while they are inexperienced in sex life and are still in the process of adjusting. To do so might be repulsive to one or both on the grounds that it would offend their aesthetic values. It is better for a couple to refrain from intercourse during the first menstrual period after the marriage. It is normal and good for them to stimulate each other to orgasms without intercourse during the menstrual period. However, having said this, it is our duty to state the fact that modern doctors agree that there is no biological harm done by having intercourse during the menstrual period. If either husband or wife thinks that they should not, then they should not. One reason for bringing up this subject is the fact that often the wife has her highest sexual desire before, during, and after her menstrual period. If the Creator made her thus, and He did, He must have meant for her need to be satisfied under the right circumstances. The menstrual flow is usually rather heavy the first day or two after which it slackens considerably. Some couples wait until the heavy flow is past and then proceed with normal sex relations.

In spite of good planning, our research reveals that the menstrual period is present on the wedding day in 17 percent of cases. When this happens, it is recommended that couples wait until after the period is past before they have intercourse. However, they should get acquainted with each other and arouse each other to orgasms through interstimulation. Actually there is some advantage in the presence of the menstrual period on the honeymoon. It allows the couple to become somewhat used to each other and to be more relaxed by the time they are able to have first intercourse.

A seventh and final question, "Is it necessary to use artificial lubrication in sexual intercourse?" All women by nature are provided with a natural supply of lubrication which flows from the walls of the vagina and from small glands located between the labia minora near the opening of the vaginal passage. Normally, this natural lubrication flows freely when a woman is highly aroused sexually. The higher the arousal, the greater the flow. Some women seem to have lubrication in abundance while others seem to have a shortage. In our research only 15 percent of wives had ample natural lubrication from the beginning. Some used artificial lubrication at the beginning of their marriage, but ceased using it because the natural flow of lubricant was sufficient. However, 34 percent of wives indicated that after six months to two years of marriage that they still had to use artificial lubrication, both for the stimulation of the clitoris and for sexual intercourse. Just as some women are tall and some are short, so some women have more natural lubrication and some have less. Whatever the amount, it is normal for that person. If there is a slight stinging or burning during direct stimulation of the clitoris or during sexual intercourse, this simply means that there is a shortage of lubrication. We recommend that couples take a tube of surgical jelly (usually called K-Y Jelly) on their honeymoon and use it freely in first sexual experiences. If a couple finds that they do not need artificial lubrication, they would, of course, cease using it. Some couples will need to use some artificial lubrication all of their married lives. However, in case of an excessive shortage of natural lubrication a woman should consult her doctor.

CHAPTER 5

The Honeymoon:
First Sexual Experiences

> *For this cause shall a man leave father and mother, and shall cleave to his wife; and they twain shall be one flesh. Wherefore they are no more twain, but one flesh. What therefore God hath joined together, let not man put asunder.*
>
> Matthew 19:5-6

THROUGH THE YEARS it will be a blessing to any married couple to have the lingering memories of a happy honeymoon. This present discussion is planned to help a couple think through their honeymoon and to help them make the most progress possible in sexual adjustment.

A couple should plan the last few days before their marriage so that they will both be feeling good mentally and physically on their wedding day. Even though last-minute wedding plans have to move at an inhuman pace, couples would do well to get good sleep during the days which precede their wedding. It is better to have a wedding ceremony as early in the day as possible. If there is a formal reception, it will take approximately two hours from the time the wedding ceremony begins until the couple is in their car, alone, and ready to travel. On the first night, it is probably better to travel approximately one hour, or just enough to find a private motel out of the reach of curious and mischievous friends. When a couple plans to spend their honeymoon 200 or more miles away, they should travel only 40 or 50 miles the first night, then travel leisurely the rest of the way the next day. If after a strenuous wedding day, they travel four or five hours after dark, they will probably be fit only for a hospital stay, rather than a pleasant honeymoon, which they so richly deserve.

When a couple arrives at the motel, it might be well to go in, lie down, and rest for a while, say 30 minutes, and then to go out and eat some food, if a restaurant is available. Usually, on the wedding day, meals are somewhat irregular. When the couple arrives back at the motel, it is normal and right for them to proceed with their first sexual experience that afternoon or night, that is, unless they are extremely tired. If either the bride or groom or both of them are completely exhausted, they should admit it and wait until the next day for their first sexual experience. In this case, it is better to secure a room with twin beds, undress privately in the bathroom, go to bed in separate beds, and sleep. If they get into the same bed, neither would sleep and what they need is good sleep.

Several couples in the research sample have volunteered the information that they went ahead with sex

relations on their wedding night because they thought
they were supposed to do so. The experience was disap-
pointing and a relative failure, simply because they were
exhausted physically. Each couple would say, "If we had
it to do over again, we would wait until the next day."
However, generally, most young people are strong and
hardy and missing a little sleep does not bother them a
great deal. Many couples feel good on their wedding
night. Our research shows that when they arrived at their
motel on their wedding night, 9 percent of the couples
were extremely tired and fatigued, 28 percent were
somewhat tired and fatigued, 35 percent were feeling
fair, and 28 percent were feeling excellent. It is much
better psychology for a couple to come to their wedding
ceremony feeling as good as possible and for them to go
ahead with their first sexual experience that day.

It is the purpose of this discussion to reduce a
couple's wonders, tensions, and anxieties on the wedding night to a minimun. But regardless of counseling
and other careful prayerful planning, couples will probably have some inner anxieties and tensions on their
wedding night. Most couples do in varying degrees. On
the wedding night both bride and groom ought to approach their first sexual experience in the following
attitude: "Sweetheart, I am so thrilled that this is our
wedding night. I have anxiously looked forward to this
hour with you for a long time and now that it is here, my
happiness can scarcely be described in words. But I
must frankly admit that I am not too certain about how
well I will do. So, if I appear to be a little nervous, and if I
do not do my part very well, will you please forgive me?
I'll do better as time goes on." If both have this type of
humble attitude, they will tend to give each other self-
confidence. Above all things, neither should be critical

of the other on their wedding night.

The following suggestions may be helpful. There must always be privacy, complete privacy, during any sexual experience. It is important to have locked doors, drawn shades, and reasonable assurance that there will be no interruptions. Privacy is especially necessary for the wife. It is very difficult for her to concentrate on her sexual arousal in a situation where her privacy is limited.

On the wedding day, it is recommended that before a couple attempts sexual relations, that they open their Bible and each of them read aloud one after the other, a specific passage that they have selected in advance. After reading these two passages, both should then kneel down beside the bed and both should audibly lead in prayer, one after the other, asking the Lord, in simple, sincere language to lead them in their lives together. This is a humble, serious period, and rightly so. When they have finished prayer, the atmosphere should gradually shift to a spirit of laughter and gaiety. There is no need to hurry. Enjoy the new relationship! Yes, have fun!

Whether or not a couple takes a bath on the wedding night is a personal decision. Assuming that they have taken a bath during the day of the wedding ceremony, it would not be necessary to take a bath before attempting sex relations on the wedding night. During married life it is good for husband and wife to bathe just before sex relations. However, taking a bath often does not fit into the circumstances just prior to sexual experiences. When a couple have the habit of taking a bath at a stated time every day, it would not be necessary to bathe just before sex relations. It needs to be emphasized, however, that in the sexual love life of marriage, *cleanliness is next to godliness*.

It may be that the best approach to the first sexual experience on the wedding day is for a couple to begin by simply undressing each other. By this is meant that the wife should take off her husband's clothes, piece by piece, and he would take off her clothes piece by piece. It is normal for them to completely undress in each other's presence in the light on the wedding night, if they can and want to. This is in harmony with Genesis 2:24-25 which says, "Therefore shall a man leave his father and mother and cleave unto his wife . . . and they were both naked, the man and his wife, and were not ashamed."

It should be pointed out, however, that some brides find it is not so easy to undress completely the first night. The reason for this is that society has taught girls to be modest and protect themselves with clothing. This is right and proper. Nonetheless, it may be a considerable shock to some brides when we suggest that it is well for them to undress on the first night of marriage in the presence of their new husbands. It must be remembered that pushing a button called the wedding ceremony does not automatically undo the feeling of modesty that has gradually developed over a period of 21 years or longer. Of the couples in our research sample, 80 percent of the brides did undress in the presence of their husbands on their wedding night and 20 percent did not. When filling out the questionnaires later, one-half of the 20 percent stated that they would undress on the first night if they had it to do over again. Actually it is not important whether a bride undresses completely the first night or a few nights later.

What to do about this is a topic of concern for most young couples planning marriage. These suggestions are simply meant to say that it is normal for young couples to undress completely the first night, if they want to and can. What a couple does about this is their own personal decision. We feel that the young husband should respect the feelings of his bride in this matter. He should not be critical of her if she hesitates. If he is patient with her during this period of adjustment, her love, respect, and devotion for him will be greatly increased and strengthened. Usually, the problem of undressing presents little or no difficulty for the young husband.

Let us assume that undressing as described above is a normal procedure on the wedding night. After undressing, it would be well for the couple to talk freely, ask and answer questions, and spend some time getting acquainted with each other's bodies.

SUGGESTIONS CONCERNING SEXUAL INTERCOURSE

When a couple is ready for their first sexual experience, there are two approaches that may be considered. The first approach is for the couple to attempt to do everything right and complete in their first sexual attempt. This includes (1) getting contraceptives ready, (2) the long love-play period in which the husband controls himself and the wife is stimulated and aroused near an orgasm, (3) and the actual sexual intercourse during which it is hoped that the wife will have her orgasm and the husband will have his orgasm with her or following her. This is such an involved and complex experience that it is unrealistic to expect couples to succeed in the whole process the first time they try.

Some readers may ask, "What problems are involved? What would go wrong?" Several things may happen. Couples will not be too sure about how to use contraceptives. They will not know just how much arousal the wife should have before they start intercourse. The young husband will be "quick on the trigger" and may reach his orgasm much sooner than he meant to have it.

The following things in first intercourse may keep the wife from having her orgasm. First, she is usually not aroused enough before starting intercourse. Second, if there is tightness or pain when first intercourse starts, she may lose what arousal she had. Third, when her husband has his orgasm first, this often stops further arousal for her. However, *a couple should not be discouraged if their first experience is not perfect*. What we have described is to be expected for most young married couples. Each time an attempt is made, the couple will learn something and will likely do better next time. Seventy percent of our research couples advise other young couples to follow this first approach — an attempt to do everything right and complete including intercourse and orgasms on the first night. However, 30 percent of the couples in the research recommend that couples follow a second approach which will be described presently.

It is well for us to think through, in detail, the procedure of first intercourse. It is best to get contraceptives completely ready first. This should be a part of the beginning love-play period. (Details on the use of contraceptives are in Chapter 6.) When contraceptives are ready, the couple would then have a love-play period as described in Chapter 4. One method of approach would be for the wife to lie on her back on the bed with knees apart and with her feet flat on the mattress and pulled up near her hips. Her husband will lie on her right side with his left hand under her head and neck. As previously stated, the husband will gently fondle, massage, and stimulate all the erotic zones of his wife's body. This includes kissing her lips and breasts and using his hands and fingers to explore and stimulate her total body, including her inner thighs, her labia majora, her labia minora, the opening of her vagina, and finally her clitoris. However, this foreplay period should not become a routine mechanical process; variety is meaningful. The wants and needs of one woman may very considerably from another. *Couples must not underestimate the significance and importance of this arousal period.* The actual purpose of this part of love-play is for the husband to arouse his wife until she is fully ready for intercourse. When she thinks she is fully aroused, she should signal her husband verbally so he can shift and start intercourse. During her first few sexual experiences, the wife may not know when to signal. In the first part of marriage, it will have to be a guess on her part. However, she will soon learn through experience when to signal the shift from the love-play period to intercourse. A major problem for many couples is that the highly aroused husband starts intercourse too soon.

When she signals, the husband will move from her right side down to the foot of the bed in front of her. She will open her feet and knees wider and he will move his body between her knees and over her body. The weight of his body will rest, not upon her, but upon his elbows and knees. This position leaves the husband and wife in a comfortable position where both of them can move their bodies freely and at will. It is necessary to point out that in this shift, the wife's level of sexual arousal may go down somewhat. This is to be expected.

In first intercourse, there should be ample lubrication including the use of some surgical jelly, and the husband should attempt entrance very carefully. When initial entry to the vagina is made, he may stop a moment to rest for the purpose of self-control. At this point, communication to each other is in order. If there is pain at this first entrance, this will cause the wife's sexual arousal to go further down. In fact, her concern and anxiety over this first experience may cause her arousal to go down considerably. After his slight rest, the husband should carefully move the penis on into the vagina. It should not be forced too far. It is well to rest again for a moment to give the husband control. Then begin movement of the penis slowly and gently to and fro in the vagina. At this point, the husband should use an iron will to keep his self-control. The wife should turn her mind and emotions loose. She should concentrate on such ideas as, "This is it," "This is my wedding night," "I've looked forward to this for a long time," "God has wonderfully planned this to be part of my life," and other similar thoughts. She should concentrate on the clitoris, the vagina, and the rhythm of the penis moving back and forth. Also, she should not worry about her husband. He will take care of himself. She may need to concentrate on herself. This does not mean that she is selfish.

Our research shows that after six months to two years experience that 82 percent of wives could become aroused and reach their orgasms while giving part of their attention to their husbands. Even after many months of experience, it was necessary for the other 18 percent to concentrate on themselves alone. In the first experiences it is well for the bride to concentrate on herself alone. The husband could stop movement briefly at intervals in order to control himself as long as possible. The wife will try to move her arousal back up to where it was before entrance and on up to an orgasm, if possible. If she has an orgasm, this will probably move her husband into his orgasm with her immediately. This much success on the first night is rare indeed. If she does not have an orgasm, (and 9 out of 10 do not in their first attempt), eventually her husband will have his orgasm without her. Often a young husband will have his orgasm in first intercourse immediately upon entry or very soon thereafter. He may even have it in the love-play period while he is arousing his bride. In our research, 45 percent of husbands stated that they had reached unplanned orgasms a few times or several times while in the process of arousing their wives in preparation for sexual intercourse. In a similar manner 27 percent of wives stated that when their husbands had them fully aroused that they had reached orgasms before the planned intercourse could take place. Neither husband nor wife should be embarrassed when this happens. The problem here is simply a matter of timing, which will improve with experience. The goal is for both the husband and wife to experience orgasms.

On the other hand, the research showed that after the husbands had fully aroused their wives by direct stimulation, that 37 percent of the husbands occasionally needed further stimulation from their wives to improve their erection and readiness for intercourse. This does not mean that these young husbands were undersexed. It simply means that in their unselfish concentration on arousing their wives for a considerable length of time, their own arousal had subsided.

Couples should face the fact that complete sexual success on the wedding night is nearly impossible, but this is nothing to worry about. What usually happens in first intercourse is that nine times out of ten, the husband has an orgasm and the wife does not. In order to think it through, let us assume that this happens. Then what? The bride must *not* feel that there is something wrong with her, that she is undersexed. She is not. God is

efficient. He does not make mistakes. The groom should
not feel that he is inadequate. He is not. He is a normal
young man. Both should remember that their bodies are
timed differently, that they are inexperienced, and that
sexual intercourse is a rather complex procedure. Let us
illustrate. Suppose neither husband nor wife could swim
and had never been in the water. Suppose they read a
book on how to swim and a teacher gave them oral
instruction on how to swim. Does this mean that they
could jump into the water and swim perfectly in the first
attempt? Naturally not! They would sink. They would
have to learn how to swim gradually. They would sink
many times before they learned to swim well. It takes
time to put into practice instructions on how to swim.
However, the person who has instruction on how to swim
and follows these instructions will progress more rapidly
than one who has no instructions at all.

In a similar manner, it takes time to put information
received in pre-marriage counseling into effective practice. Most youth, in dreaming about sexual fulfillment in
marriage, tend to think that all they have to do is to be in
love, get married, and have intercourse, and that they will
automatically drift off into a ninth heaven of sexual
ecstasy. *Nothing could be more false*. In marriage, they
will both drift off into a ninth heaven of sexual ecstasy
hundreds and hundreds of times, but this does not happen by accident. It results from intelligent planning,
initiative, cooperation, understanding, practice, and
love, combined with experience.

Thus, a couple must not be discouraged if first
intercourse is not completely successful. They should
not allow themselves to worry about it. But rather, they
should laugh at their "goofs." Each time they "goof" (and
they will do this many times across the years) they can

simply laugh and say, "Well, we 'goofed' tonight, but we learned something and we will do better next time." Actually, during first intercourse a couple will learn much even though it is not fully successful.

Now, if the husband has an orgasm and if the wife does not have an orgasm in the first intercourse on the wedding night, then the husband, after a brief rest, should attempt to arouse his wife again and bring her to an orgasm by direct stimulation of the clitoris. This procedure will be discussed presently.

SEXUAL INTERSTIMULATION

Before discussing further attempts at intercourse, let us discuss a second procedure that may be used on the wedding night. The couple may decide not to attempt intercourse the first night, but instead, will attempt to get acquainted with each other and to stimulate each other to orgasms by direct stimulation of their genital organs. There are two advantages to this approach. (1) A couple does not have to use contraceptives, and there is no worry about a possible pregnancy. (2) This would tend to give them the best possible mental attitude and relaxation in their first sexual attempt. (Also, this is the procedure they would follow when the menstrual period is present on the wedding night.) Only 15 percent of couples in the research sample followed this approach. But another 15 percent of the couples stated that if they had it to do over again they would use this approach. Note that the couples had been counseled to consider using this approach.

Now let us discuss in detail this second approach in which a couple would *not* attempt intercourse the first night, but would attempt to gradually get acquainted with each other and stimulate each other to orgasms. It is a part of the wife's education for her, soon after marriage, to get acquainted with the nature of her husband's erect penis, how it may be stimulated, what his orgasm is like, how much semen there is, etc. Since the husband is quickly aroused to an orgasm, it may be well for his orgasm to be first. Usually, there will be little or no problem involved in the wife stimulating her husband to an orgasm. She will gently stimulate his penis with her hands and fingers until he has an orgasm. She will simply observe what happens. This knowledge and experience can be very meaningful to her.

After the husband has rested briefly, he will then attempt to stimulate his wife to an orgasm by gently stimulating the erotic zones of her body, including her clitoris. The young husband needs to get acquainted with the nature of his wife's clitoris, how to massage it, and to observe the general nature of her arousal and orgasm. This is a part of his education. In our research sample 40 percent of the wives had their first orgasm by direct stimulation of the clitoris and later learned how to have orgasms in intercourse. Since 40 percent of wives *may* have to have their first orgasm by direct stimulation, regardless of how they approach the first night, let us carefully review details of this process.

Assuming that the husband has had his orgasm, he will now have no problems of self-control and can concentrate on arousing his wife. After a reasonable amount of kisses, body stimulation, and love-play, the wife will lie on her back on the bed and the husband will gently stimulate her clitoris with his fingers, remembering that her clitoris may be very tender. With the dry finger stimulating the dry clitoris, there could be some stinging and burning. The husband may transfer some lubrication from his wife's vagina to her clitoris. If there is a need, the husband will use a generous amount of surgical jelly as artificial lubrication. As stimulation continues, the wife should concentrate on her arousal, turning herself, her mind, and her emotions loose. In fact, it may take intense mental concentration on her part.

The young husband should think in terms of stimulating both the clitoris and the area around and close to the clitoris, including the inner lips and the hood (point where the inner lips meet). During the initial stages of the stimulation, the husband can usually feel the clitoris with his fingers. However, as the wife becomes more fully aroused, the inner lips and the hood will increase in size until he can no longer feel the clitoris even though he is continuing the same type of direct stimulation. Although he cannot feel the clitoris, the husband should simply continue this same process of stimulation, as it gives the clitoris efficient *indirect* stimulation and continues the arousal process of the wife. Since a husband cannot read his wife's mind, it is well for her freely to give him verbal instructions concerning the type of direct stimulation that means the most to her arousal. As her needs change, she should shift her instructions. At times she may want the stimulation to be extremely gentle and delicate. At other times she may want the stimulation to include some pressure. With some experience both will soon learn to respond to the processes necessary for her arousal.

Sexual feelings may be very meager for the wife at the beginning of the arousal period. As the stimulation continues, pleasant sex feelings will gradually grow, build up, develop, and rise higher and higher. This should be continued for 5 minutes, 10 minutes, 20 minutes, 30 minutes, an hour, or longer, if necessary. This must be uninterrupted stimulation. If stimulation has continued for 10 minutes, if the wife is to the highest possible level, usually called the "plateau" stage, and if the stimulation is interrupted for one minute, her arousal will go down quickly. So, the stimulation must be uninterrupted, 10 minutes, 20 minutes, 30 minutes, etc. When the wife is aroused near an orgasm, she will begin to breathe a little faster, heavier, and deeper. Sometimes a wife may get close to her orgasm but it may seem difficult for her to move on into it. But, if they will simply continue this arousal procedure, eventually it will happen. *Many couples fail to bring the wife to an orgasm simply because they stop the arousal procedures before the wife is fully aroused.* The *right attitude*, the *right technique*, and *persistence will succeed*.

Sometimes her sexual feelings will seem to come and go. Now she has it — now it is gone. Sometimes the build-up comes in waves, each wave getting a little more intense. These waves gradually get closer together until the last one "flows over the top," which is the orgasm. At other times instead of the sexual arousal coming in waves, there is a gradual continuous sexual build-up to the orgasm. As a wife moves into her orgasm, her faster, deeper breathing, her mental concentration, her intense sexual ecstasy will culminate in a slight jump of the body, and a short quick gasp for breath. This is the orgasm. This is actually a muscular explosion, an extremely pleasant spasm of the clitoris, the vagina, and all of her body from the top of her head to the bottom of her feet. Her body, arms, and legs stiffen, she breathes still faster, heavier, and deeper, and she shakes inside and out with waves of pleasure for 6 or 8 long fast deep breaths which take only 15 seconds or less. It may be that the most intense sexual enjoyment in this process of having an orgasm is the period just before the stiffening of the body and the final fast deep breathing.

The orgasm is ended by a sigh, a smile, relaxation, and deep appreciation to her husband for giving her so much joy, and making it possible for her to express her God-given nature, which is a wonderful part of the blessing of being a woman. A woman's orgasms may vary in intensity from time to time, depending on the circumstances. It is obvious that it would hardly be possible for a woman to have an orgasm without knowing it. The husband usually does know when his wife has an orgasm, but at times he may not. He may not know during the first few experiences. As soon as his wife is experienced in having orgasms regularly, he will know all of the time. Under no circumstances should the wife fib to her husband and tell him that she had an orgasm when she did not. This could set up problems that are difficult to overcome. It is better for husband and wife to face total reality together from the beginning and work things out together. After a young wife has had some orgasms, she soon learns what procedures to follow in order to succeed regularly.

One couple in the research sample had this experience. They attempted intercourse on their wedding night and the wife did not have an orgasm, but the husband did. After intercourse, they attempted to bring her to an orgasm by direct stimulation. In the process she gradually became tense, nervous, and just could not continue the arousal effort, although she tried and wanted to do so. She had to ask her husband to stop the stimulation. They lay there, relaxed, and talked for over three hours, on into the night. Finally, long after midnight she said, "I want us to try that again." They repeated the process of direct stimulation, and after about 17 minutes she reached her first orgasm. What actually happened, in her case, was that she learned much in her first effort and after becoming relaxed and more confident, she was able to give herself fully to sexual arousal and thus succeeded.

A couple should not be worried if the wife does not have an orgasm at the first attempt. In the research 29 percent of wives did experience orgasm the first time they tried on their honeymoon, either in intercourse or by direct stimulation. Please note that 71 percent of wives failed to have an orgasm the first time they tried on their honeymoon. However, 79 percent of wives had one or more orgasms by the end of the honeymoon or the end of one week. It took two weeks for some couples and two months for others. At the end of six months, a few wives had not yet had orgasms. Some of them succeeded in approximately one year. These figures giving the experiences of 151 couples should mean two things to a bride and groom. First, they need not be discouraged if they do not have perfect sexual fulfillment at once. Second, all couples can and will eventually succeed if they persistently apply the proper techniques in a loving, patient, and understanding attitude toward each other. If a couple has been married three or four months and the wife has not yet had an orgasm, they should seek the help of a marriage counselor. Appendix V gives information on how to secure a marriage counselor. In our research, all couples who returned to me for additional help soon succeeded in their adjustment. To seek help does not mean that a couple admits defeat, but rather it says, "We refuse to be defeated." Actually, it may be that we have made this process of sexual adjustment in marriage appear harder than it really is, but we have done so willfully in order to help couples under all circumstances, just in case it should be needed.

Actually there are three steps in sexual adjustment that couples need to learn. They are as follows: first step — orgasms, second step — orgasms in intercourse, third step — orgasms together or close together in intercourse. It will be remembered that in our research 60 percent of wives had their first orgasms during intercourse. For them the first two steps came together. This should be the goal of all couples. However, let us remember that 40 percent of wives in our research had to have their first orgasm by direct stimulation. This does not mean that there is anything wrong with those wives. They are not undersexed. It is simply a matter of learning. Some couples learn a little faster than others.

At this point, let us consider the 40 percent of wives who had to have their first orgasm by direct stimulation. After learning how to have orgasms by direct stimulation, sometimes there is a little difficulty in learning how to achieve orgasms in intercourse. It takes a little time and practice to learn this procedure. Some suggestions may be helpful. (1) Take more time in the arousal period. (2) See that the wife is more highly aroused before starting intercourse. (3) Shift quickly from the arousal position to intercourse. (4) The wife should continuously and intensely concentrate on her goal — arousal and orgasm — during intercourse. (5) The husband should attempt to prolong intercourse and respond to his wife in the movements and procedures that she wants, needs, and enjoys.

After trying one or two months, if the wife can have orgasms by direct stimulation but cannot get to an orgasm in intercourse, it is then wise and necessary for the wife to have further direct stimulation of the clitoris while in the process of intercourse. When a couple starts intercourse after the regular arousal period, they may choose one of two ways to give further direct stimulation of the clitoris. One way is as follows. After the arousal period and immediately after intercourse is started, the husband may place the weight of his body on his left arm, put his right hand down on his wife's clitoris, and give her further direct stimulation while intercourse continues. This is somewhat awkward, and couples cannot kiss during this process, but it can be done and is effective. Twenty-four percent of couples in our research sample indicated that they had used this technique successfully. Usually with two or three minutes of this kind of final stimulation, the wife will move into her orgasm in intercourse. She can signal her husband as she moves into her orgasm, and he can drop into the regular position and can have his orgasm either with her or immediately following her orgasm.

There is a second way in which this extra stimulation may be achieved. After the arousal period and as the husband shifts to start intercourse, the wife may put her finger on her own clitoris and continue giving herself the same direct stimulation that her husband has been giving her. This keeps her arousal from going down during the shift. The husband shifts and starts intercourse. He must give his wife enough room between their bodies to keep her hand on the clitoris. After a few minutes of this process, the wife can move into her orgasm and her husband can move into his orgasm with her, or immediately following her. Of the two methods, this second procedure is the most comfortable and may be the most efficient. But some wives have a psychological block at the thought of stimulating their own clitoris and thus cannot use this procedure successfully, but do enjoy using the first procedure. For the wife to stimulate her clitoris to hold her arousal level up while her husband shifts and starts intercourse should not be thought of as an evil procedure. This is a total cooperative husband-wife relationship. Remember the illustration of the piano-violin duet! Since male and female bodies are different, sexual adjustment calls for both husband and wife to do the right thing, at the right time, and in the right attitude. If there is need for a wife to have further direct stimulation after intercourse begins, the couple should not hesitate to give it to her in the way most satisfactory to her.

In sexual adjustment, one thing is important to a couple; namely, both husband and wife should enjoy orgasms in sexual intercourse when intercourse is possible. The method of stimulation and arousal used is not so important, so long as it reaches the ultimate goal for both. Of course, the method used must be mutually acceptable and agreeable to both.

Often couples ask, "Can we learn to have our orgasms at the same time in intercourse?" The answer is that husbands and wives who have had careful counseling and who cooperate fully with each other can gradually learn to have many of their orgasms either together or close together. Our research shows that after six months to two years or marriage experience, 36 percent of the couples were having their orgasms at the same time, either most of the time or all of the time. Forty-three percent had had orgasms together a few times; whereas, 21 percent had not yet experienced their orgasms at the same time.

Most modern marriage counselors agree that the traditional assumption that husband and wife must have simultaneous orgasms is false and must be rejected. Certainly, they would agree that it is not as important that man and wife have orgasms together as it is that *both have orgasms*. However, it is excellent for couples to work toward the goal of having orgasms together or close together. The best procedure is for the couple to plan for the wife to have her orgasm first and allow the husband to follow with her, or *immediately* after her, as he can.

Many counselors advise that the wife have her orgasm first and be through it just before the husband starts his. The advantage of this approach hinges on the fact that when the husband and wife are in their orgasms they are in a state of semi-consciousness and can do little or nothing by way of helping the other, or being aware of what the other is doing or experiencing. Thus there may be some advantages to this approach (separate orgasms — the husband following immediately after his wife) to both husband and wife. The husband can consciously help his wife into her orgasm and through it, and in the process, he can consciously enjoy her experience. By the time she is through her orgasm, she can now consciously help her husband into his orgasm and through it, and can consciously enjoy his experience. This should be very meaningful to both of them.

We recognize that there is much truth in the reasoning that having orgasms, one following another, is advantageous, and we agree that this approach is completely satisfactory. However, we would not agree that this approach is superior to the procedure where both husband and wife move into their orgasms at the same time. When husband and wife have their orgasms at the same time, it seems to offer them both a plus, a dividend, a zenith of spiritual oneness, emotional joy, and physical ecstasy. It leaves nothing lacking. Actually, either approach is fully satisfactory. To compare these two methods is about like comparing identical diamonds or identical twins.

In this connection, there is often the problem of the husband getting to his orgasm before he planned to, and before his wife gets into hers. With time and experience the husband can usually bring this problem under control. If he does get to his orgasm first, the wife should continue toward her orgasm. She should not stop. The husband should continue regular movement, helping her as much as possible. He should not speak to her nor in any way break her concentration in the final approach to her orgasm. From the time the husband crosses the line toward his orgasm (where he cannot turn back), until he is finished, is approximately a minute or longer. During this time, often the wife can continue and sweep herself emotionally into her orgasm with him or following him.

In pre-marriage counseling conferences on sexual adjustment, some couples ask, "What do you do when intercourse is finished?" Usually, couples remain in the same position, leaving the penis in the vagina for two or three minutes or longer as their sexual experience gradually subsides. This period is normally filled with hugs, kisses, and love pats, expressing affection for each other. After a few minutes, the penis is withdrawn and the couple lies side by side in each other's arms fully relaxed. They continue conversation with endearing words of appreciation and happiness. Actually, *this period of "afterglow," expressing affection after intercourse, is very important*. If this period is enjoyed by both husband and wife, it is evidence that their relation is not simply interest in physical sexual expression, but that it is a relationship of true love and spiritual oneness. This indicates a good marriage adjustment. The Christian concept of "one-flesh" is thus realized.

CHAPTER 6

Controlling Parenthood Through the Use of Contraceptives

I have no greater joy than to hear that my children walk in truth. 3 John 4

Our Heavenly Father, we thank Thee for Thy foreseeing providence, that Thou didst love us in Christ from the foundations of the world. May we share in Thy planning for our lives by sharing in Thy foresight for the children Thou wilt give us. Purify our hearts of irresponsibility and self-love, even when it poses as obedience to Thy laws. Help us to bring the discoveries of science under the dominion of Thy sovereign Grace. For Thou hast not made anything common or unclean. All things are for Thy glory. Amen.

Wayne E. Oates

YOUNG COUPLES planning marriage are vitally interested in planned parenthood and they have a right to be informed on the subject. There are two types of information needed. First, couples need information that will help them to approach marriage with the proper attitude concerning the use of contraceptives. Second, they need information on the efficiency of specific types of contraceptives and how to use them. It was established in Chapter 2 that the Creator planned two functions for sexual intercourse in marriage. The procreative function is for reproduction and the propagation of the race. The unitive function is for the husband and wife to express, nourish, and develop their love for each other. It is futile to argue over which of these two functions is the most important. Certainly, neither one of them can be considered secondary. It is better to think of them as equals. Both are important and necessary in the plan of God for marriage.

Since sexual intercourse has two distinct functions, certain problems arise. When a couple has intercourse for the purpose of planned procreation, it is accompanied with the unitive function of love expression and there is no problem. However, in the unitive function of intercourse for love expression only, as planned by the Creator, there is always a possibility of pregnancy, and thus a problem arises. Since God created husband and wife with a continuous need of sexual expression, it follows that there would be one pregnancy after another, unless some effort is made to control it. Twenty to 25 children for one couple is unthinkable. Also, it is unthinkable for husband and wife to refrain from sexual intercourse except for procreation. Just as man used his mind to invent a hoe to keep weeds out of the corn, so it is necessary for him to use his mind to make certain that the two God-created functions of sexual intercourse be allowed to operate, without abusing or destroying each other. The modern birth control movement is simply a human effort to allow both functions of sexual intercourse to operate normally. Thus, through the use of contraceptives, husband and wife personally can plan for parenthood according to their needs, and at the same time can have regular sexual expressions of their love through the pleasure of intercourse.

The Bible gives no positive or negative statement on birth control. The story of Onan in Genesis 38:8ff. cannot be used objectively as evidence opposing birth control. When Onan's older brother Er died, his father Judah instructed Onan to marry Tamar, the wife of his deceased brother, and to raise up children to her. This practice was regular among the Hebrews. It is called the "levirate." When Onan had intercourse with Tamar, he practiced "coitus interruptus," that is, he withdrew before orgasm, spilling the semen on the ground. When he refused to raise up children to his brother's wife according to the Hebrew custom, he was put to death. His sin was not that he wanted to have intercourse for pleasure without reproduction, but rather that he refused to carry out his moral duty to his deceased brother, according to Hebrew law.

Most major religious denominations have either officially approved the intelligent use of contraceptives, or some of their agencies have voiced approval. The Southern Baptist Convention, for example, has not officially approved or disapproved the planned parenthood movement. At a Southern Baptist Conference on Family Life, one workgroup's findings stated:

Without hesitation or apology, we endorse the principles of planned parenthood. We believe each family has the right to seek and to receive information on birth control in order that children may be planned for and wanted

when born . . . We, therefore, urge that the Christian
Life Commission publish and circulate findings of Baptists and other groups which promote responsible
parenthood *(The Church and the Christian Family*,
Nashville, Tenn.: Convention Press, 1963, page 114).

Generally, Baptists and several other evangelical
groups have followed the point of view that the use of
contraceptives is a private personal matter to be decided
between husband and wife. The fact remains that most
of the members of these groups believe in and practice
the use of contraceptives. They are not violating any
official regulation of their denomination. A young Christian couple may marry with the confidence that they
have, not only a positive responsibility to God and themselves to have one or more children, but that they have a
positive responsibility together in determining the
number and spacing of children. Also, they may marry
with confidence that the intelligent use of contraceptives
for the spacing of children and making possible regular
sexual intercourse for love expression is definitely within
the framework of the plan of God and basic Christian
principles.

CONTRACEPTIVES COMPARED

The most commonly used birth control methods,
listed in order from the most effective to the least effective — giving the number of unplanned or unwanted
pregnancies in one year per 1,000 women (properly
using each method) and the approximate cost (Federal
Drug Administration Bulletin, February, 1973) — are as
follows:

1. The most effective is the (Estrogen and Proges-
   tin) *pill*, with one pregnancy per 1,000 women,
   costing approximately $1.50 to $3.00 per
   month.

2. The second most effective is the *vasectomy* (the cutting of the male vas deferens by a minor surgical operation) with two pregnancies per 1,000 couples, costing approximately $100 to $300.

3. The third most effective is the *condom* (a rubber sheath, sometimes called a prophylactic) used *with a contraceptive jelly or cream* with ten pregnancies per 1,000 women, costing about 40 cents per use.

4. The fourth most effective is the *intrauterine device* (IUD), with 19 pregnancies per 1,000 women, costing about $15 at the time of insertion.

5. The fifth most effective is the *diaphragm plus a jelly or cream*, with 26 pregnancies per 1,000 women, costing approximately $10 at the time of fitting plus approximately 15 cents per use for jelly or cream.

6. The sixth most effective is the *condom without cream*, with 26 pregnancies per 1,000 women, costing approximately 25 cents per use.

7. The seventh most effective is *vaginal foam*, with 76 pregnancies per 1,000 women, costing about 15 cents per use.

8. The last and least effective is the rhythm method, with 140 pregnancies per 1,000 women, with no cost except for the 140 women who become pregnant.

ORAL CONTRACEPTIVES

Before discussing the use of traditional birth control methods, a word about the new oral contraceptives is in order. When taken according to medical instructions, the oral contraceptive pills now on the market are almost 100 percent effective in helping a couple control parenthood. It is true that there are some physical side effects involved in using the pill, and some women refuse to use it for this reason. However, to see the possible side effects in perspective, the death rate from using the pill is 22.8 per 100,000 women as compared with 100 deaths per 100,000 who have illegal abortions. The use of the pill is less of a hazard to life and health than is smoking, driving an automobile, or swimming.

The author is inclined to encourage young couples to consider using oral contraceptives under the direction of their trusted personal physician. Certainly it is well for all couples to thoroughly discuss the possible use of oral contraceptives with their physician before making a final decision concerning the type of contraceptives to use. It should be remembered that a physician positively will not prescribe oral contraceptives under certain health conditions. One of our major concerns is to help young couples enter marriage under circumstances which will promote efficient sexual adjustment in marriage as early as possible. The use of oral contraceptives largely removes fear of pregnancy and the complicated problems involved in the use of conventional contraceptives. Other things being equal, this is, indeed, a major advantage. Assuming no ill effects on human health, we may safely say that there are no more moral grounds for questioning oral contraceptives than there are to question the approved traditional contraceptives.

THE CONDOM PLUS VAGINAL JELLY

Of the traditional contraceptives used, the condom plus vaginal jelly is probably the most efficient and satisfactory during the first months or years of marriage.

They are easy to purchase at any drugstore, do not require a prescription, and are simple to use. The condom is a rubber sheath that fits over the penis to receive the semen and keep the sperm cells out of the vaginal tract. It is the most widely used traditional contraceptive. Vaginal jelly contains a chemical that destroys sperm cells on contact. It is inserted into the vagina and deposited near the mouth of the womb with a plastic applicator. Many couples trust the use of the condom alone. However, when circumstances require planned parenthood, the use of vaginal jelly with the condom gives added protection. By rigidly following instructions when using both the condom plus vaginal jelly, the risk is very small.

In using the condom, the husband should spread a small amount of surgical or vaginal jelly, or other lubrication (Remember! a *very small amount*) on the head of the rigid penis. It is well to unroll the dry condom about one and one-half rolls and stretch it over the head of the penis, being careful not to get the lubrication on the condom except on the inside at the very tip. The tip of the covered penis should be massaged briefly to lubricate the condom at the top on the inside. Then the dry condom should be rolled down over the dry rigid penis as far as possible. The small amount of lubrication at the head of the penis is for the purpose of allowing the condom to stretch rather than to bind, which might cause it to break. Before first sexual intercourse, the top two-thirds of the outside of the condom should be lubricated. When the dry condom is stretched over the dry erect penis and lubricated on the outside, it will not slip off during intercourse movement.

A condom should be carefully checked before it is used to be sure it is not defective. Condoms purchased at drugstores are made under government supervision and inspection. Supplies are kept fresh. This makes possible reliable merchandise. It is true that the use of a condom may slow down sexual sensation for the husband. However, since most young husbands are sexually "quick on the trigger," the use of a condom is a definite advantage in that it gives some extra needed control in the early part of married life. Condoms are so thin that they will dull sensation very little and will not prevent a husband from reaching a normal orgasm at will. After orgasm, when the erect penis has gone down, the husband should withdraw carefully lest the penis slip out of the condom and leave it in the vagina. There is the possibility of this leaving sperms in the vagina. To avoid this risk, the husband should lift his body up with hands and arms and the wife should reach down and hold to the penis and condom as he withdraws. This will always withdraw the condom with the penis.

Normally, it is best for the couple to get contraceptives completely ready before the arousal period starts. When using vaginal jelly, it is strongly recommended that the jelly be inserted into the vagina at least ten minutes by the clock, before the husband's orgasm takes place. During this time the body temperature will melt the jelly and it will run into all areas of the vagina, thus increasing protection. However, the ten minutes is not a problem because a couple ought to take this much time and more in the arousal period. When vaginal jelly is used with a condom, the condom should be examined carefully after intercourse. If there has been no problem, then the vaginal passage could be washed out at will. However, if there is a question as to the effectiveness of the condom, then the jelly should be left in the vagina for eight or ten hours before washing it out.

The vaginal passage, by nature, keeps itself clean and does not need to be washed out except under the direction of a physician. However, when foreign material is put into the vagina, such as vaginal jelly, it may need to be washed out. Some doctors recommend the bulb douche and others recommend the fountain syringe. The bulb douche is in one piece and is the least trouble to use. It can be wrapped in a towel and easily carried while traveling. The fountain syringe is made up of a two quart rubber container and a long rubber tube, with nozzle. It is a little more complicated to use, but its gentle washing action is to be considered. Many physicians feel that the fountain syringe is the most efficient in thoroughly cleansing the vagina. A woman should follow the advice of her doctor. Either instrument may be purchased at any drugstore. In washing out the vagina, lukewarm water is sufficient. Do not use other preparations unless directed by a doctor.

Condoms should be purchased only one or two dozen at a time. When kept too long, their resistance to breaking may decline. Condoms may be reused successfully. Although it is more expensive, most couples feel that it is more satisfactory to use a new one each time. A used condom when washed out and dried can be rerolled by stretching it over two fingers and slowly rolling it with the other hand. The chances of an accident are considerably greater when reusing condoms. Condoms should not be disposed of through the toilet, as they will clog the sewage system.

THE INTRAUTERINE DEVICE (IUD)

Another method of birth control is the intrauterine device, usually called the IUD. It is a soft, flexible plastic loop or irregularly shaped disc which a physician must insert through the vagina and the cervix into the uterus. This can be done in any doctor's office with a minimum of discomfort and is rarely painful. The IUD may cause some cramps and backaches a few days after insertion; there also may be a heavier-than-normal menstrual flow or even some spotting between periods for the first several months by the user of this device. However, approximately 90 percent of women have no trouble with the IUD. A woman using the IUD should carefully follow her doctor's instructions and should be checked by her doctor approximately once a year. For those women who can use the IUD without any complications, it can be one of the most convenient means of controlling birth.

The Diaphragm Plus Vaginal Jelly

Another highly approved contraceptive is the use of the diaphragm plus the use of vaginal jelly. This method is recommended by many physicians. The diaphragm is a flexible rubber disk that is placed in the vagina over the cervix (the opening between the vagina and the womb) to prevent sperms from entering the womb. A woman must be fitted for a diaphragm by a physician. The size of the vaginal passage varies among women, and it is important to use the right size diaphragm in order to have the most protection. After fitting the diaphragm, the physician will teach his patient how to insert it into the proper place for maximum efficiency. In intercourse, the penis in the vagina moves back and forth underneath the diaphragm. Neither the husband nor the wife will be conscious of the presence of the diaphragm during intercourse, if it is in the proper place. If a couple, having used the diaphragm and jelly have had intercourse once and attempt it again after several hours, a second application of vaginal jelly

should be used for maximum protection. After intercourse, the diaphragm and jelly should be left in the
vagina for 8-10 hours. Then the vagina may be washed
out as described above. If a couple has intercourse in the
daytime, the wife would need to wear a pad until time to
wash out the vagina.

One advantage of the diaphragm is that the wife can
insert it before time for sexual arousal. However, the
jelly should be inserted just before the arousal period
starts. Another advantage is that the diaphragm gives the
husband maximum stimulation. Let us repeat, that usually the young husband does not need more stimulation,
but less, in order to control himself while waiting for his
wife to be fully aroused. Most physicians will not fit a
young bride-to-be with a diaphragm because of the hymen, and because the handling of the condom is a little
easier and a little more certain for beginners.

Some doctors and marriage counselors recommend
that couples begin married life by using a condom plus
vaginal jelly and that they later shift to the use of a
diaphragm plus jelly. This presents a psychological
hazard to some young couples, especially when they are
anxious to control the time of parenthood. Some may
reason that they are using the condom successfully and if
they change, they have no assurance that they can use
the diaphragm successfully. Therefore, we recommend
that newly married couples continue to use the condom
plus jelly to a point of six months before they are ready to
begin their first pregnancy. At this point, if both husband
and wife agree, they could shift to the use of a diaphragm
and vaginal jelly under the direction of a physician. If a
pregnancy should result, they will welcome it. If they use
the diaphragm and vaginal jelly six months without a
pregnancy, they may be reasonably certain that they can

use it successfully, and thus they will have conquered the psychological barrier of changing contraceptive methods. They can cease using any contraceptives to start a pregnancy and, after the baby is born, can resume using the diaphragm with considerable confidence. The cervix is somewhat larger after the birth of a baby. Therefore, a wife should go back to her physician after each pregnancy and be refitted for a diaphragm before resuming sexual intercourse.

The manufacture and sale of contraceptives is a major business. Through the normal processes of competition, many companies have products on the market. We may be certain that some of this advertised merchandise is substandard. A young couple planning marriage should follow the advice of their physician or marriage counselor in selecting brand names of contraceptives. A wise couple would not order and use contraceptives that are newly advertised in some off-brand magazine, guaranteeing 100 percent efficiency. Neither would a wife use a strange contraceptive just because a neighbor lady had been using it successfully. It is possible that the neighbor lady might be a person for whom it is difficult to effect a pregnancy or she might even be sterile without knowing it. If there are effective contraceptives available, the doctor or marriage counselor will know about it and will recommend them.

The subject of contraceptives should be discussed, and decisions should be made by a couple a few weeks before the wedding date. In general, the decisions of a couple should be the result of free discussion and a harmonious agreement between the two. Many of us feel that the husband would want to be sure that the wife approved the method of birth control used, since it is the wife who bears the major responsibility in reproduction.

It is obvious that the use of some contraceptives is a rather complex, messy, and unaesthetic procedure. This causes some young people to have a psychological block and to rebel against the use of contraceptives, a problem that is not present in the use of the oral contraceptive pills, the IUD, or vasectomy. However, since some couples must use conventional contraceptives, it is helpful for them to fuse the preparation of contraceptives with the love-play arousal period. Gradually the use of contraceptives can become an acceptable part of the total love experience.

Young couples need to be informed that there is a possibility of a pregnancy when the husband does not have an orgasm. When the penis is erect, there is a fluid that seeps from the urethra (the opening in the penis) in all men. In some men (10-15 percent) loose sperm cells get into this fluid. It is very difficult to determine when these loose sperm cells may be present. Many factors are involved, such as health, the duration of time between sexual experiences, etc. Sometimes, when husband and wife retire at night, during endearing conversation, they become sexually aroused. Although they do not plan orgasms, they may place the penis in the vaginal passage for a while, relax, and go to sleep. This is a normal and pleasant experience, but there is the possibility of a pregnancy, even without an orgasm. Couples who need to control birth should avoid placing the penis in the vaginal passage except when contraceptives are used. When a couple is within six months of the time when they would like to begin a pregnancy, they could practice the above-described procedure once or twice a week and especially during the ovulation period. To do this without a pregnancy occurring would present some evidence that they could practice this love experience in the future with less risk. However, it should be stated that some risk is always present. Perhaps it would be profitable for a couple to discuss this with their physician.

One form of birth control which is not recommended by marriage counselors is "coitus interruptus," that is, withdrawal of the penis before orgasm takes place. There are two major objections. First, there is little assurance that this method of control will work. The possible loose sperm cells described above would be a hazard to some. Furthermore, the nature of sexual arousal for a man is such that he probably will not have accurate control of his behavior just prior to orgasm. The second objection is the psychological effect of withdrawal on the sexual experience of both wife and husband. This method calls for abrupt interruption right at the precise moment when both need continued and even stepped-up movement and stimulation in order to give full expression to the God-created love experience planned for them. The withdrawal may deny the wife her orgasm in intercourse. Couples are concerned about two things, planned parenthood and good sexual adjustment. To practice coitus interruptus gives them neither one.

Two couples in our research sample practiced a different type of control. They were exceedingly anxious to finish their education. During the first month or two of their marriage, they lived in mortal fear of a pregnancy until the menstrual period appeared each month. Finally, they mutually agreed as a temporary policy not to have intercourse, but rather to express their love and sexual need in simultaneously bringing each other to orgasms by direct stimulation. Although they were looking forward to the day when they could freely have intercourse, they indicated that their temporary procedure was fully acceptable and satisfactory, under the circumstances. Few marriage counselors would recommend this procedure. However, most of them would agree that it was realistic planning on the part of the two couples, in their specific circumstances.

Another method of planned parenthood not recommended by most marriage counselors is the "rhythm method" or the so-called "free period," that is, avoiding sexual intercourse three or four days before and after the ovulation period. It is assumed that during the rest of the monthly cycle, conception could not occur. There are several reasons why this method of control is unreliable. Medical science is not yet certain about the length of life of either the sperm cell or the egg cell. Also, it is difficult to determine the exact time when ovulation takes place. Normally, in a 28-day menstrual cycle, it is expected to be at the end of the fourteenth day, that is, the fourteenth day before the beginning of the next period. Our research indicates that since their marriage, 60 percent of the wives did not follow 28-day cycles. Ten percent had cycles shorter than 28 days and 50 percent had cycles longer than 28 days. Furthermore, before their marriage, 45 percent of wives in our sample had irregular cycles. After their marriage 47 percent of wives had irregular cycles. The average length of their menstrual cycle before marriage was 31.2 days. After marriage it averaged 30.1 days.

Even if a cycle is somewhat regular, this is not a guarantee that the ovulation period will be on the fourteenth day. Women are not mechanical automatons. They are persons with feeling, motivation, a desire for happiness, and inclinations toward self-protection and self-preservation. Many life experiences, such as a disease, a crisis, an accident, or a disappointment may shift the ovulation period a few days. Also, some women ovulate on the stimulus of sexual intercourse. In other words, the so-called "safe period" is not reliable. This is not to say that a couple would never use this approach. Certainly, couples whose circumstances demand planned parenthood would not use it.

When a couple is within six months of the time that they plan to effect a pregnancy, they could experiment. They could study carefully the pattern of the wife's menstrual cycle and locate the ovulation period, insofar as possible. They should carefully use contraceptives for four or five days on each side of the assumed ovulation period, but could run some risks during the rest of the cycle. If a pregnancy results, it would be lovingly welcomed, since this was planned. If conception did not take place after six months of experimenting with the free period, then it could be assumed the ovulation period was regular enough to run some risk in the future. However, the percentage of risk would still be rather high. The consciousness of willful risks is not conducive to happy sexual relationships.

It is well for every young wife to keep a permanent calendar record of the beginning date of her menstrual period. This record will be helpful in planning and avoiding conception in her married life. Also, this record will be meaningful as a part of her medical record, for her doctor as he gives her medical supervision. A calendar record remembers, whereas it is easy for the mind to forget.

Many young couples show considerable anxiety about the process of purchasing contraceptives at the drugstore. Some suggestions are in order. Let us assume that this responsibility belongs to the husband. He should write down on paper the specific items desired, including the brand names of condoms, vaginal jelly,

etc. On entering the drugstore, he should look for the
druggist. The high school age young people who work at
the soda fountain normally do not sell contraceptives. In
two or three times out of five, a woman clerk will attempt
to wait on the young husband. He may say to her, "I want
to see the druggist." When the husband gets to the
druggist — who could be either a man or a woman — or
any older clerk in the store, it is not necessary to say
anything. He may simply hand the druggist the list as one
would a prescription. Immediately, the druggist understands the nature of the purchase and will secure the
items on the list, and the merchandise will be wrapped in
a package. Thus, the purchase is completed, often in the
presence of other customers without their knowing the
nature of the transaction.

Although we have assumed that the husband would
purchase contraceptives, there is no just reason why the
wife should not make such purchases. If there is no older
woman clerk available, she would hand her written list to
the druggist who will complete the transaction in an
impersonal, dignified, and businesslike manner. There is
really no justifiable reason why a young couple should
hesitate to purchase needed supplies. This is a normal
procedure experienced by the druggist many times per
week. It may be helpful for a couple to purchase supplies
from a druggist or clerk who is a personal friend.

It is obvious that in using contraceptives, there is a
greater possibility of an accident during the first sexual
experiences of married life. Therefore, in order to control
birth, a couple should plan carefully after securing the
best advice possible. They should remember that no
physician or marriage counselor is infallible. The human
element is always present. The responsibility rests upon
the joint decision of the couple. Although a couple

should not allow the possibility of effecting a pregnancy to become a major source of fear, they should plan and proceed carefully. They should reason and make decisions in light of known truth, but proceed in the frame of mind that if a baby should result from this love experience, it would be fully accepted, fully loved, and be given the same opportunity for total life as if there had been positive plans.

Notes

[1]Federal Drug Administration Bulletin, February 1973.

CHAPTER 7

A Study of Poor Sexual Adjustment in Marriage

The husband should give to his wife her conjugal [sexual] rights, and likewise the wife to her husband. For the wife does not rule her own body, but the husband does; likewise the husband does not rule over his own body, but the wife does. Do not refuse one another. . . .

1 Corinthians 7:3-5 (RSV)

A MARRIED WOMAN who has not experienced a sexual orgasm wants to know, and rightly so, why she has not had the experience. What are some possible conditions which could prevent her from having orgasms? Usually it can be said that there would not be any one single cause, but rather *many small interrelated causes* working together that explain why a wife has not achieved orgasm. If a couple can locate these possible causes, understand them, and accept them as real, they are halfway to victory. These causes may be outlined as follows:

I. A CONFLICT RELATIONSHIP BETWEEN HUSBAND AND WIFE

1. There may have been conflicts between the husband and wife during their courtship days which have been carried over into married life. During courtship, these conflicts may be played down or ignored, but in marriage they tend to grow and become very real. They may consciously, or unconsciously, block a good love relationship.

2. There may have been conflicts or misunderstandings on the honeymoon in the initial stages of sexual intimacies. These could cause lingering emotional scars and more conflict.

3. There may be further conflicts in other areas. Five or ten years difference in age may cause unconscious disagreement and strife. If a husband feels that his mother, sisters, or relatives are better cooks or housekeepers than his wife, this could be a major source of conflict. Differences in other areas, such as education, finances, religion, social life, and cultural background may cause conflict.

4. There may be secret dislikes for each other's habits, attitudes, ideas, and tastes which could tend to block an effective love relationship.

5. There may be a feeling of competition or jealousy between husband and wife, instead of a feeling of mutual reciprocal love, trust, and confidence.

II. PERSONAL PROBLEMS OF THE HUSBAND

1. The husband, who often has a very strong sex drive, and normally so, may tend to be selfish in seeking sexual satisfaction. It is difficult for him to comprehend the slow arousal nature of his wife. Most couples who

have not developed a happy adjustment do not take enough time in the arousal period. The husband's hasty approach may unconsciously be crude, bold, and tactless, instead of an approach characterized by gentleness, kindness, patience, tenderness, understanding, and humility.

2. Sometimes an insecure husband is a dominating husband. No human being likes to be dominated. If a husband tends to dominate his wife, this develops in her secret fears that may block their love relationships.

3. A few young husbands go into marriage with secret fears about their own sexual capacity, such as feeling they are undersexed, their penis is too small, or that they will not be able to satisfy their wives. Most of these fears are purely imaginary and have no basis in fact. Yet they are real in the minds of some young husbands and they may hinder a man from meeting the total sexual needs of his wife.

4. There may be strong guilt feelings about the past such as compulsive masturbation or other attempted sexual outlets.

III. Personal Problems of the Wife

1. The young wife may have developed inner fears about sex which root deep into her childhood and youth experiences. This is sometimes caused by a lack of proper parental guidance. Often, girls secretly feel they are undersexed because their sex drive is not manifested as is that of boys or some exaggerated, imaginary stories they have heard about the sex lives of some women. It is common for girls to feel that they are undersexed. Actually, they are not. God does not create undersexed persons.

2. Sometimes young girls enter marriage with as-

cetic ideas, i.e., they feel that sex is not "spiritual," that nice girls just don't "stoop to such." This *utterly false* and *unchristian* idea can easily block a woman's sexual progress in marriage. Her parents and society have failed to help her understand and distinguish between two facts: (a) sex life in marriage (monogamy) according to the plan of the Creator in nature is both moral and spiritual, and (b) only the *misuse* and *abuse* of sex is evil. (Gen. 1:27-31; 2:18-25; Mark 10:9; Prov. 5:1-21; 1 Thess. 4:1-8; Heb. 13:4; 1 Cor. 7:1-5, and all of the Song of Sol.).

3. The rather long period of physical unpleasantness during the first days and weeks of sexual experience in marriage may condition the young wife against sex or crystallize some of her secret fears. This physical unpleasantness may include such things as failure to succeed in inserting the penis into the vagina for several days, some bleeding when entrance is made, and considerable pain during the first efforts at intercourse. In our research sample 52 percent of wives indicated that they experienced slight pain at first intercourse, while 28 percent indicated considerable pain during first intercourse. Out of 151 couples, 63 couples stated that it took three to nine sexual experiences before the pain ceased. Seventeen couples stated that it took from 10 to 25 sexual experiences before this pain ceased. These are simply biological realities. Although they are unpleasant, they actually have no relation to a woman's capacity for normal sex life.

4. Some girls go into marriage with major feelings of insecurity and inferiority. These feelings tend to block sexual adjustment. Lacking self-confidence, young women are often too passive to become aroused to a full sexual experience.

5. Sometimes girls go into marriage with guilt feelings about the past. During teenage years a driving curiosity leads some girls to limited experimentation. Guilt feelings about this experimentation may condition their minds against sex.

6. Sometimes a wife is simply happy with things as they are. Her main concern during courtship was marriage, a husband, a home, and a baby. Now she has them all. She is thrilled with her life situation. She enjoys meeting her husband's sexual needs. She enjoys her home, her baby, and her friends. She lives unselfishly for them and simply neglects her own sexual needs.

IV. OTHER GENERAL PROBLEMS

1. In a few cases it may be a health problem, such as a poor diet, hormonal deficiency, or glandular disturbance. Most of these problems can be corrected by skilled medical guidance.

2. Some couples simply get into marriage with a lack of knowledge about the nature and function of the sexual organs and about normal sexual techniques. This would not be true of many college graduates or others who have had thorough pre-marital counseling by a qualified marriage counselor.

3. One of the major hindrances to sexual adjustment in marriage is the lack of time for sexual experiences. Many couples hurry . . . hurry . . . hurry through life and through their sexual experiences, for lack of time. It is difficult for a young wife to give herself fully to a sexual experience with her husband during hurried circumstances.

4. Equal with the lack of time is the lack of privacy, which is often experienced in the first part of married life. Unlocked doors, curtainless windows or doors,

squeaking beds, and thin walls are problems. These problems can generally be solved by a couples' creative ingenuity. For example, many couples have made pallets on the floor in order to avoid squeaking beds.

5. Some couples, before marriage, assume that perfect sex adjustment in marriage would be easy, quick, and automatic. When this does not happen, they develop fears, guilt feelings, and often panic. They become over-anxious, are too serious, and try too hard. In their determined effort to succeed, they often antagonize each other. They need to realize that their experience is rather universal, and that it may take weeks and months to effect good adjustment.

Throughout this book, the author has pressed the thesis that good sexual adjustment in marriage is of major importance. By definition, good sexual adjustment occurs when both husband and wife are dedicated in love to meeting each other's total spiritual, emotional, and sexual needs and when both have orgasms during each sexual experience in expressing their love to each other. The method of arousal, the position used, the time involved, and the frequency of experiences are of secondary importance. These may vary from time to time and from couple to couple.

Efficient mutual sex life for husband and wife should tend to produce many positive fruits. (1) It should develop individual inner self-confidence. (2) It should release much energy to be utilized in absorbing creative projects outside of oneself, involving others in the home and community. (3) It should tend to promote security, maturity, happiness, and general personality development. (4) It should promote better physical health. (5) It should help present the right family environment for growing children, that is, a mother and father in a happy love relationship. (6) It should tend to develop the moral and social fiber of the community by decreasing extra-marital sex relationships and divorces. A community with strong family life should be able to develop an efficient social structure. (7) Last, but not least, good sexual life between husband and wife should tend to develop a close, warm, personal, spiritual relationship between them and God.

It must not be assumed that an emphasis on good sexual adjustment in marriage means that such an adjustment guarantees happiness in marriage. Every marriage counselor is acquainted with many cases where couples had good sexual adjustment but whose marriages were characterized by quarreling, conflict, emotional struggle, separation, and divorce. In order to have happiness in marriage, all of the phases of total life experience (the spiritual, the mental, the social, the emotional, the moral, the physical, and the sexual) must work as a cooperative unit. However, we must not fail to understand that in God's plan for married life good sexual adjustment is of major significance.

Some have asked, "Can all women achieve sexual orgasms in marriage?" The answer is "yes . . . if." A significant percentage do not achieve orgasm. In fact, 10 to 12 percent of married women in society do not achieve orgasm. However, as a result of our eleven-year research findings, we contend that all women can achieve orgasm in marriage; that is, if they (1) do not have a biological handicap which prevents orgasms (which is very rare), (2) are in reasonably good health, (3) do not have some major mental or emotional disturbance, (4) are in a reasonably good marriage relationship, and (5) apply the principles, attitudes, and techniques advocated in Chapters 2, 4, and 5, then the answer will probably be *yes*. All women can learn love expression in sexual orgasms. Thorough pre-marriage counseling on sexual adjustment in marriage is of major importance in helping women to realize this high ideal.

Others have asked, "If women can achieve sexual orgasms in marriage, does it not follow that God created men and women to be equals, sexually?" A "yes" answer seems to be necessary. Although they are different in the manifestation of their sexual needs, it is well for us to think of men and women as equals sexually, that is, equals in capacity and equals in spiritual and physical satisfaction. God created both man and woman "in his image." He created them to supplement each other, to complete each other. This is equality. In 1 Corinthians 7:2-5 (see Chapter 2), Paul describes the sexual relationships of husband and wife. The central thought of this passage is that they are equals sexually.

In the past it has been assumed that man was superior sexually. This assumption was based upon man's relative quickness and woman's relative slowness in sexual arousal. It is false reasoning to assume that slowness or quickness in timing constitutes sexual superiority or inferiority. Modern research and thought on sexuality have rejected the old concept of the superior male. Our research showed that the men of the sample would like to have intercourse every 2.7 days and the women every 3.2 days, and that 61 percent of women wanted a sexual experience as often as their husbands did or more often. The fact that some men may want sexual experiences more often in the first part of life is overbalanced by the fact that some women may want sexual experiences more often in the years past middle age and menopause. Thus, couples would do well to think in terms of man and woman being equal sexually.

The idea of sexual equality is very helpful in the process of working out a good sexual adjustment in marriage.

A wife who has not achieved sexual orgasms in her marriage is usually in an unfortunate situation. In her sexual experiences with her husband she is sometimes slightly aroused, but never satisfied. Secretly she is disappointed but does not admit it. Sexually, she had expected much in marriage and rightly so, but she has received little. She is careful to help meet her husband's sexual needs, but secretly wonders if there is something wrong with her. As the weeks pass into months, and the months pass into years, the same pattern prevails — slightly aroused, but never satisfied. Gradually she becomes nervous, irritable. The experience becomes distasteful to her. She puts it off as long as possible. When she does submit, it is routine, formal, mechanical. She still loves her husband, but her love is not in the one-sided sexual experiences. This affects the husband's experience. It is not at all satisfactory for him. Unless they are both rather mature Christians, they may drift into a twilight zone of conflicts, frustrations, and emotional scenes. Small molehills may be expanded into mountains. There may be conflict over how to spend their money. Relationships with in-laws may become a major problem. As time moves on such a wife falsely imagines she is undersexed. She feels rejected sexually. She fears that she cannot command her husband's love. She becomes suspicious and jealous. Her husband becomes restless, ill-tempered, impatient, and sullen. When this type of husband-wife relationship is allowed to continue across the months and years, only tragedy can result.

If a Wife Has Never Experienced Orgasm

Any couple who has been married three to six

months and has not adjusted sexually should make positive plans toward achieving good adjustment. They must take the initiative. All marriage counselors are familiar with couples who achieved success after one, two, ten, twenty, or more years. It is always obvious that these couples succeeded because they were *trying* to succeed. On the other hand, marriage counselors are familiar with people who have not succeeded and it is obvious that they *have not tried* to succeed.

Any married couple who has not achieved sexual adjustment must set out on a carefully charted plan in which together they move in the direction of victory. Both husband and wife will have to get a fresh start as if they were just now getting married. The past must be forgotten, and each must give the other a chance to perform without demand or criticism. Both should be very clean, and the husband should have a fresh shave and his fingernails trimmed and smooth. All sexual attempts should be in a very private, warm place with no chance for interruption. Both should be rested and as free as possible from stress and tension. The effort is logically divided into two periods of time involving progressive types of sexual arousal techniques.

During the first period, involving approximately one week, sexual effort would be as follows: Both husband and wife should take off all their clothing, and the husband should use his hands and fingers to touch, massage, and fondle his wife's body anywhere she lovingly directs him, while she simply relaxes and becomes conscious of the pleasure gained from his caresses. The wife should avoid any thought of hurrying or of any feeling of need to satisfy her husband, or any effort to experience her own orgasm during this time. Both husband and wife should avoid negative ideas, such as "I am inadequate"; "I am undersexed"; "I am ugly"; "God is punishing me"; "My parents neglected me"; and "Society has rejected me." They should think positive ideas, such as "God is infinite and good"; "Sex is God's idea"; "I have qualities, abilities, and talents like other people"; "Sex is a central part of me"; "I must use all that God has given me (including sex) to develop my personality and grow spiritually"; "We are equals"; "We need each other"; and "We must meet each other's needs."

The couple should repeat these unhurried, relaxed times for whatever period of time that gives the wife pleasure — for at least one week. During this period they would avoid touching each other's genital organs. During these sessions, the wife is learning to enjoy her husband's caresses and what her body needs and that she does respond to loving stimulation.

Following the above practice sessions, the wife should now be ready for more intense arousal, moving toward maximum sex pleasure. This should involve all of her body, including her genitals. The next sessions during the second period involves the following procedures: Probably the best position for the couple to use (as described in Chapter 5) is for the wife to lie on her back on the bed with her knees wide apart, her feet pulled up near her hips, and her feet resting flat on the mattress. Her husband should be on her right side with his left hand under her head (Song of Sol. 2:3; 8:3). This position allows the husband freedom of access for creative exploration and stimulation of her entire body. As the husband explores her body, the wife should place her hand slightly on his so that she can encourage him in specific directions, with the amount of pressure needed to meet her "where and how" desires at any particular time or place. This will allow both husband and wife to learn precise physical communication without verbal request or detailed explanations. The wife should direct his every movement, and he should refrain from any of his own ideas as to what may be stimulating to her. Most women seem to achieve much more pleasure by well-lubricated stimulation along the sides of the clitoris, the inner lips, and around the opening of the vagina. Rarely is there pleasure in introduction of fingers deeply into the vagina.

In these sessions, there should be no hurry, and the wife should not at this point attempt to force herself to reach an immediate orgasm. These sessions should extend over a period of several weeks, two or three times per week. Each week the couple will learn a little more about how to excite the wife sexually. A wife should avoid feelings of fear or dread; fear must be banished because "There is no fear in love" (1 John 4:18). She should think in terms of adventuring, seeking, exploring, giving, and receiving. A couple should be content to learn a little at a time. As the weeks move by, the couple will gradually move closer to success. Success depends equally on husband and wife. At any time during these efforts that a wife is highly aroused sexually, she should try to continue increasing the intensity of the stimulation with his hand or her hand until she experiences an orgasm. (The nature of the orgasm is explained in detail in Chapter 5.) The wife should feel complete freedom to stimulate her own clitoris area, if needed, to produce her first few orgasms. Her role in this process must be active, not passive. Both husband and wife must be persistent. Both should be conscious of the fact that this kind of lovemaking in marriage is completely within the will and plan of God and is pleasing to him (Gen. 2:24, 25; Prov. 5:18, 19; Song of Sol. 2:3; 8:3; 1 Cor. 7:2-5). After a wife succeeds in experiencing several orgasms in the above manner, the couple should follow the procedures outlined in Chapter 5 in relating the wife's experiencing orgasm to sexual intercourse and meeting her husband's sexual needs.

(The above paragraphs on the topic "If a Wife Has Never Experienced Orgasm" have followed some of the ideas on the cassettes *Sex Problems and Sex Technique in Marriage* by Dr. Ed Wheat, M.D., Springdale, Arkansas. Used by permission.)

Confidence in themselves and confidence in and love for each other is important. By all means, a couple should make it a matter of prayer. We should remember that sex originated in the infinite mind of God, that it is God's creation, and that it is God's plan that it be central in all of our lives. Mutual sexual experience in marriage is the focal point of love expression between husband and wife. It tends to relieve anxiety, lessen guilt, and prevent the formation of conflict, tension, and hostility. Also it tends to increase and fortify love and affection. Unquestionably, it is an experience that gives inner poise and security.

Sexual expression in marriage is a function of the total personality at the highest and deepest levels. It makes possible tender understanding, communion, and communication between husband and wife that cannot be expressed in language. Through one-flesh sexual experiences in marriage, the spiritual and the physical unite in their highest and most pleasant relationship. Husband and wife are sublimely fused into complete unity and identity through their one-flesh sexual experiences. Truly, sex is the servant of marriage and of Christianity.

APPENDIX I
Description of Research Methods

Our research on sexual adjustment in marriage involving 151 couples grew out of teaching marriage and family classes in sociology, as described in Chapter 1. The plan was to give couples thorough pre-marriage counseling on sexual adjustment in marriage and to follow through with a detailed questionnaire to measure the degree of sexual adjustment after marriage.

Couples voluntarily requested pre-marriage counseling. The counseling involved three separate steps. A few weeks before the wedding date they were given the book, *Sex Without Fear*, by Lewin and Gilmore (Medical Research Press) and instructed to read it separately. After reading the book, they were given the *Sex Knowledge Inventory* test, form X. This test contains information concerning sexual adjustment in marriage. Finally, the couple came to the home of the author, where in privacy he sat down across the table from them and spent an average of 2½ hours giving them details on sexual adjustment in marriage. Each conference was opened with prayer. Often during the conference, passages from the Bible were used to help the couple understand that the techniques being described were based upon Christian concepts. The counseling routine used in the conference is printed in Chapters 4, 5, and 6. The conference was planned to discuss in detail, ideas and problems that could be expected to cause some wonder and anxiety as the couple looked forward to marriage. They could ask questions at any time. Often, couples came with some anxiety, but they soon relaxed and entered freely into the spirit of the conference. At the end of the period, the couple would drift into relaxed conversation with the counselor on the subject of sex as it related to Christian life and to their future experience together.

When there were no more questions to ask, the counselor would speak to the couple as follows: "This conference is my wedding present to you. Under no consideration can you pay me anything for this service. Now, I want to ask a favor of you. Without realizing it, when you came for counseling, you became a potential member of my research sample. When you have been married six months, I want to send you a detailed questionnaire that will measure your experience in sexual adjustment. When you have carefully filled in the questionnaire together, and mailed it back unsigned, then I will mail you a copy of my findings without expense.

"You see, it is very difficult to secure objective information on this subject. Let us imagine that we had never met, and were complete strangers. Suppose that after you had been married six months, I came to your door and stated that I was a sociology professor from a certain university, that I was doing research in family life, and that I wanted to talk to you about your sex life. You would probably firmly shut the door in my face, and rightly so.

"But this is a different situation. You came to this conference at your own request. Both of you know me as one of the college professors. You have been in my sociology classes. I have taken considerable time to help you in matters that vitally concern you. We understand each other's interests and motives. Our relation as Christian friends is such that you can trust me to keep in strict and complete professional confidence information you would give me about your own sexual life. This type of relationship between counselor and counselee would enable you to give frank, objective, and accurate truth about your experience. This kind of research is extremely valuable. The best source of information about sexual adjustment in marriages is the experience of couples who have recently been married. For you to participate in this research will not only be helpful to you personally, but you will be joining me in a major research project that should be of future service to many other fine couples like you."

Every couple which was counseled agreed to cooperate in the research, and 98 percent filled in questionnaires. As the questionnaires came in, temporary tabulations were made of the first thirty-three and later of the first hundred. The findings were used in improving the counseling routine and are central in this book. It would be impossible to separate the counseling and the research. They developed together in the experience of the counselor and the couples counseled. This fact makes the study somewhat unique.

Out of the 151 couples in our sample, 98 percent were church members, 92 percent were Baptists, 83 percent of husbands and 96 percent of wives had attended Sunday school regularly in childhood and youth, 76 percent of husbands and 79 percent of wives had been Sunday school teachers, 73 percent had regularly given a tenth of their income into their church, 86 percent (of the couples) read from the Bible and prayed audibly together on their wedding night, 90 percent practiced regular family worship, 90 percent had a prayer before meals, and 96 percent of husbands and 93 percent of wives led public prayer in church activities. It is probably safe to generalize that 90 to 95 percent of the members of the sample were active, consecrated Christian individuals.

APPENDIX II
Research Findings

Percentages and Averages from Questionnaires Filled in Six Months to Two Years after Marriage by 151 Couples Who Had Been Given Pre-Marriage Counseling, Outlined in Chapters 2, 3, 4, 5, and 6.

Instructions for interpretation of these findings: In interpreting the following percentages, averages, and other findings, couples should be careful in comparing their own experiences with these figures of this survey. An average is not necessarily the norm. Sex varies in men and women just as tallness and shortness varies. Neither tallness nor shortness would be considered abnormal. These findings may be helpful to any married couple. They may assist counselors in guiding couples who need help or couples who are planning to be married.

1. Did you ever discuss and seriously consider the possibility of a secret marriage?

    Yes 8.0%   No 92.0%

2. How long before your marriage did you begin to discuss frankly together personal attitudes and rather complete details about sex?

    23.5% before engagement

    26.8% immediately after engagement

    18.8% six months before marriage

    20.8% three months before marriage

    8.1% one month before marriage

    1.3% one week before marriage

    .7% not until the honeymoon

3. Did you have any experiences in childhood and youth that impressed your growing mind that sex was evil or distasteful?

Husband	Yes 30.2%	No 69.8%
Wife	Yes 33.3%	No 66.7%

4. Were you taught by your parents, either by implication or by direct language, that engaging in pre-marital sex relations was wrong?

Husband	Yes 88.2%	No 11.8%
Wife	Yes 93.4%	No 6.6%

5. Did either of you feel any discomfort or embarrassment during the counseling period with me because of our frank and detailed discussion of sexual adjustments in marriage?

Husband	None 84.2%	Slightly 15.8%
	Considerable 0.0%	
Wife	None 75.7%	Slightly 22.9%
	Considerable 1.4%	

6. Did the counseling conference give you information with which you were not acquainted?

Husband	None 2.8%	Very little 11.2%
	Some 48.3%	Much 37.8%
Wife	None .7%	Very little 6.1%
	Some 53.1%	Much 40.1%

7. What subjects discussed in the counseling conference were the most meaningful to you?

A summary of replies are listed in descending order according to the number of times given in the responses.

How to stimulate and arouse wife to an orgasm

The use of contraceptives

The detailed processes of sexual intercourse

Suggestions on what to do and expect on the honeymoon

The nature of the clitoris

The different sexual timing of men and women

How to meet the husband's sexual needs

The spiritual and moral interpretation of the sexual relationship in marriage

The elimination of fears and wonders

The responsibility of husband and wife meeting each other's sexual needs

How to purchase contraceptives

The discussion of the hymen

Good sexual adjustment takes time

8. Would you recommend that other couples planning marriage take advantage of this counseling service or a similar service?

Husband	None 0.0%	Some 4.1%	All 95.9%
Wife	None 0.0%	Some 4.0%	All 96.0%

9. Did you go to see a doctor prior to your marriage concerning your marriage?

Husband	Yes 36.2%	No 63.8%
Wife	Yes 62.7%	No 37.3%

10. Did the wife prior to your marriage have a pelvic examination including the hymen, vagina, and womb?

Yes 54%   No 46%

(Note: The counselor recommended a pelvic examination to each prospective bride at the pre-marriage counseling conference.)

11. Did the doctor in giving the pre-marriage pelvic examination:

Appear hurried 21.4%

Give you all the time you needed 78.6%

12. Do you consider your experience with the doctor and the information you received prior to your marriage to be:

33.8% Very Satisfactory

50.0% Satisfactory

12.2% Unsatisfactory

4.0% Very Unsatisfactory

13. Have either or both of you seen a marriage counselor or doctor since you were married for the purpose of better sexual adjustment?

    Yes 12.4%   No 87.6%

    (Note: A majority of those who replied "yes" came back at their request to see their original counselor.)

14. If your answer to 13 is "no," have you had a feeling that you really should?

    Yes 7.0%   No 93.0%

15. Did the wife ever have a pelvic examination anytime before her marriage for medical purposes? (This does not include the pelvic examination recommended by your counselor.)

    Yes 27.1%   No. 72.9%

16. Did you see each other naked the first night of your honeymoon?

    Yes 79.2%   No 20.8%

    If yes, were there any fears or emotional problems involved?

Husband	None 87.9%	Slightly 12.1%
	Considerable 0.0%	
Wife	None 66.7%	Slightly 30.9%
	Considerable 2.4%	

17. When conditions are favorable, do you recommend that other young couples see each other naked on the first night of their honeymoon?

Husband	Yes 92.5%	No 7.5%
Wife	Yes 89.9%	No 10.1%

18. Would you advise other couples to attempt a sexual experience on the first night of the honeymoon?

	IF they are not fatigued		They are fatigued	
Husband	Yes 94.0%	No 6.0%	Yes 28.0%	No 72.0%
Wife	Yes 94.0%	No 6.0%	Yes 23.1%	No 76.9%

19. Check only one:
    84.5% (a) In our first sexual effort on our honeymoon we attempted to do everything complete including intercourse and orgasms.
    15.5% (b) In our first sexual effort we did not attempt intercourse, but in the process of getting acquainted gradually, we simply attempted to bring each other to orgasms through love play and direct stimulation.

20. Would you advise other young couples to follow —
    19a? 70.5%   19b? 29.5%

21. On your honeymoon, what was the nature of the physical complications or barriers to sexual intercourse, if any? Check those that apply.
    (a) 42.4% We could not make entrance at first attempt. For 20 couples it took 3 to 9 days for them to succeed in making first entrance. It took 6 couples from 10 to 30 days to succeed.
    (b) First intercourse was 52.3% slightly or 28.5% considerably painful for the wife. For 63 couples it took from 3 to 9 experiences at sexual intercourse before the pain ceased. It took 17 couples from 10 to 25 experiences before the pain ceased.
    (c) If intercourse was painful at first, as you look back, was it biological 47.0%, part biological and part mental (fear and tenseness) 49.6%, largely mental 3.4%.

22. We had a doctor dilate (stretch) or cut the hymen either before or after our marriage so we could have intercourse.
    Yes 13.3%   No 87.7%

23. On your honeymoon, did the wife enjoy first intercourse? Check all that apply.
    5.3% It was disappointing to me.
    4.6% I was really uncomfortable and was glad when it was over.
    22.5% Although I did not enjoy it physically, it meant much to me.
    21.2% I enjoyed it, but had some tenseness and fear.

47.7% I enjoyed it in that it was the first time that I could give myself fully to my husband.

9.9% I fully enjoyed it mentally, emotionally, physically, and spiritually. (Note: This 9.9 percent involved 15 wives, 8 of which stated they had slight pain in beginning first intercourse.)

*24. What were your anxieties, fears, and wonders on your wedding night?

31.0% None

26.7% Some apprehension and embarrassment

15.5% Some suspense and curiosity

15.5% Fear of pain

10.1% Concern for the other person

4.2% Fear of pregnancy

*25. Did you take a bath before attempting sex relations on your wedding night?

Yes 50.7%   No 49.3%

26. Do either of you have any feeling that your sexual intercourse as husband and wife may be sort of shameful or evil?

Husband   None 99.3%   Slightly (sometimes) .7%
                Considerable 0%

Wife   None 98.0%   Slightly (sometimes) 2.0%
            Considerable 0%

27. Do either of you have a feeling that your sexual intercourse as husband and wife is an act of virtue and purity?

Husband   Yes 95.9%   Uncertain 2.7%   No 1.4%
Wife   Yes 93.8%   Uncertain 5.5%   No 0.7%

28. Many marriage counselors feel that the achieving of actual physical orgasm is important and necessary, but to emphasize this alone is very misleading and inadequate. They feel that there are other deeper and more significant spiritual and non-physical meanings to a sexual experience between husband and wife. Do you agree?

| Husband | Yes 95.1% | No 4.9% |
| Wife | Yes 96.0% | No 4.0% |

29. When the wife is fully aroused and ready for intromission (intercourse), does the husband need help from the wife at this time to improve his erection and readiness for intromission?

    None 69.4%   Occasionally 27.3%   Often 3.3%

30. How often on the average do you have sexual intercourse?

    Once every 3.3 days.

31. How often would you like to have intercourse and orgasms if you could have this experience every time you really wanted to?

    Husband: every 2.7 days   Wife: every 3.2 days

32. What have been the largest factors, if any, in your experience together that have tended to hinder efficient sexual relations?

    A summary of replies are listed in descending order according to the number of times given.

    Fatigue and tiredness
    Lack of time due to busy work and study schedule
    Slowness of wife's arousal
    Difficult for husband to control self and wait for wife
    Late work and study hours
    Work causes us to retire at different times
    Contraceptives get in the way
    Lack of privacy
    Fear of pregnancy

33. During the last year the time of day that we have had sexual relations has been somewhat as follows:

    8.6% in the morning   12.5% in the afternoon
    78.9% at night

34. Approximately what percent of your sexual experiences are:

    spontaneous 67.9%   pre-planned 32.1%

35. When your sex experiences are pre-planned, who brings it up?

>   The husband 68.6% of the time.
>   The wife 31.4% of the time.

36. Since marriage:

>   96.6% We have used a double bed all of the time.
>   0.0% We have used twin beds all of the time.
>   2.7% We have used both, but use a double bed most of the time.
>   0.7% We have used both, but have used twin beds most of the time.

37. From our experience, we recommend that other young couples entering marriage use:

>   A double bed 98.7%   Twin beds 1.3%

38. Assuming privacy, which do you prefer during sexual intercourse?

	Husband	Wife
Complete light	0.8%	0.0%
Dim light	50.0%	47.5%
Complete darkness	24.6%	10.1%
It makes no difference	24.6%	42.4%

39. Does fatigue before sex relations adversely affect?

>   The husband the most   9.4%
>   The wife the most   37.0%
>   Both about the same   53.6%

40. Assuming tiredness and fatigue, but after relaxation for a reasonable length of time, do you go ahead with an enjoyable sexual experience?

>   2.4% Never
>   52.9% Sometimes (0 to 50 percent of the time)
>   25.0% Often (50 to 75 percent of the time)
>   19.7% Most of the time (75 to 100 percent of the time)

41. Assuming tiredness and fatigue, do you recommend that other couples consider going ahead with a desired sexual experience, after a period of relaxation?

>   Yes 92.3%   No 7.7%

42. Has the husband ever reached an unplanned orgasm in so far as timing is concerned, while he was in the process of arousing his wife for coitus?

   None 55.0% A few times 40.4% Several times 4.6%

43. Has the husband experienced any premature ejaculations? (This refers to quality. Question 42 refers only to timing.)

   Yes 29.0%   No 71.0%

   (Note: This 29 percent seems to be rather high. Perhaps further research is needed on this subject.)

44. For the husband:

   97.8% One orgasm is sufficient in one sex experience.

   2.1% More than one orgasm seems to be needed for each experience.

45. Is the sex experience definite now for the wife, that is, is she able to reach a definite orgasm (climax) in your sex experiences?

   Yes 96.1%   No 3.9%

46. What was the specific time from the time of your wedding until the wife first succeeded in reaching an orgasm either by direct stimulation or intercourse? (Check one)

   29.2% The first attempt during the honeymoon.

   49.6% Before the honeymoon was ended.

   21.2% She did not experience an orgasm during the honeymoon.

47. Did the wife reach her first orgasm through: (Check one)

   39.6% Direct stimulation of the clitoris without intercourse.

   50.7% Sexual intercourse after a period of direct stimulation.

   9.7% Sexual intercourse alone without any direct stimulation.

48. How often now do her attempts succeed in orgasm?
    38.6% All of the time
    57.1% Most of the time
    4.3% Less than half of the time
    0.0% Seldom

    (Note: Most of the 4.3% involved couples where the husband desires intercourse every day.)

49. Do her orgasms vary from time to time in intensity?
    None 6.5%   Slightly 84.7%   Considerable 8.8%

50. Approximately how long in minutes did it take the wife to reach her first orgasm?
    17.1 minutes (average)

51. Approximately how long on the average does it take the wife now to reach an orgasm?
    10.2 minutes (average)

52. What is the shortest length of time in which the wife has reached an orgasm?
    5.3 minutes (average)
    21.2% of wives had experienced orgasm in 3 minutes or less.
    10.0% of wives had experienced orgasm in 2 minutes or less.
    3.3% of wives had experienced orgasm in 1 minute or less.

53. For the wife:
    76.4% One orgasm seems to be sufficient to meet her needs.
    20.0% More than one orgasm seems to be needed sometimes.
    3.6% More than one orgasm seems to be needed most of the time.

54. When the wife is aroused near an orgasm, can she reach the orgasm after intromission during the process of intercourse without further direct stimulation of the clitoris?
    Yes 58.7%   No 41.3%

55. Can the wife reach an orgasm through process of sexual intercourse without being aroused by direct stimulation?
    Yes 40.4%   No 59.6%

56. Has the wife experienced premature orgasms, that is, has she, when aroused by direct stimulation, had an orgasm before the planned intromission could take place?
    None 73.3%   Occasionally 22.9%   Often 3.8%

57. Have you succeeded some of the time in reaching your orgasms at the same time in sexual intercourse?
    20.8% Not yet
    43.2% A few times
    22.3% Most of the time
    13.7% Regularly

    (Note: In the pre-marriage counseling conference, the counselor instructed couples on techniques to follow in order to have orgasms together, but indicated that many marriage counselors feel that simultaneous orgasms may not be of vital importance.)

58. If you have not reached your orgasms at the same time regularly, which one of you usually has the orgasm first?
    38.2% The wife usually is first.
    35.7% The husband usually is first.
    26.1% The procedure is varied.

    (Note: The couples were counseled that it is better if possible, for the wife to have orgasm first.)

59. While the wife is being aroused to an orgasm:
    17.6% She must concentrate on herself alone.
    82.4% She can become aroused while giving part of her attention to her husband.

60. Have there been times when the wife helped the husband to an orgasm when she did not attempt an orgasm?
    None 8.0%
    A time or two 45.7%
    Several times 46.3%

    (Note: The couples were counseled that this procedure was normal in a limited number of circumstances.)

61. Have there been times when the husband helped the wife to an orgasm when he did not want an orgasm and did not attempt one?

> None 47.1%
> A time or two 35.3%
> Several times 17.6%

(Note: The couples were counseled that this procedure was normal under limited circumstances.)

62. One technique in arriving at orgasms together is (after the wife is fully aroused through love play and direct stimulation of the clitoris) for the wife to stimulate the clitoris while the husband gets into position and starts intercourse. (Check one)

> 71.6% We have never used this technique.
> 16.2% We use this technique successfully.
> 12.2% We used to use this technique but no longer need to.

(Note: The couples were counseled concerning the possibility of this procedure when there was need for it.)

63. On intensity of orgasms in general, my orgasms are:

Husband	Wife	
0.0%	3.8%	Very mild
14.2%	29.8%	Mild, but definite and enjoyable
67.2%	51.1%	Very intense and enjoyable
18.6%	15.3%	Extremely intense and enjoyable

64. Has the wife ever had an orgasm without intercourse and without any kind of direct stimulation of the clitoris? In other words, can she sometimes arouse herself to an orgasm by the use of the mind, thinking about love and sex?

> Yes 6.3%   No 34.0%   Have never tried 59.7%

65. Counselors report that some women become sexually aroused in dreams and experience orgasms. Has the wife experienced orgasms in dreams?

> Never 86.0% Occasionally 14.0% Frequently 0.0%

66. If you have had a pregnancy, did you bring each other to orgasm by direct stimulation during the time before and after the baby's birth, when the doctor indicated that you should not have intercourse?

    Husband stimulated wife to some orgasms.
        Before 58.8%   Yes 41.2% No
        After 40.0%   Yes 60.0% No
    Wife stimulated husband to some orgasms.
        Before 71.4%   Yes 28.6% No
        After 66.0%   Yes 34.0% No

(Note: The couples were positively counseled concerning this possibility.)

*67. Does the husband know when the wife has an orgasm?
        52.9% All of the time
        40.0% Most of the time
        7.1% Sometimes
        0.0% Never

*68. Check those that apply.
        22.5% The wife gives the husband a verbal signal when she is moving into her orgasm.
        29.8% The wife gives the husband a non-verbal signal when she is moving into her orgasm.
        26.8% When the wife is moving into her orgasm she is too involved in concentrating on the experience to signal her husband.
        53.5% The husband can always tell when the wife is moving into an orgasm and does not need a signal.

*69. For the husband: Describe two or three of the wife's actions which indicate to the husband that she is having an orgasm. The husbands responded as follows:
        55% deeper, faster breathing
        47% increased movement
        35% tenseness and stiffening of body, arms, and legs
        25% more intense hugging and squeezing
        24% orgasm is followed by a deep sigh and relaxation
        15% contractions of the vagina
        5% strained facial expression

*70. In intercourse, when the husband starts his orgasm first, is the wife able to continue and sweep herself into her orgasm by the time he finishes or soon thereafter?

    6.0% All of the time
    42.0% Most of the time
    32.0% Less than half the time
    20.0% Never

71. Concerning positions in sexual intercourse: (Check all that apply)

    63.6% We use the normal position (man above) most of the time.
    1.3% We have never experimented with any other position.
    53.6% We experiment frequently with other positions, but usually use the normal position.
    4.0% We use some other position more than half of the time.
    5.3% We use some other position most all of the time.

*72. For the husband: What relationships with your wife give you the most sexual arousal? Check first, second, and third in order of the degree of arousal.

	1st	2nd	3rd	Weighted Total**
Touching	77.1%	18.6%	4.3%	191
Seeing	11.8%	58.8%	29.4%	124
Thinking	16.6%	18.2%	65.1%	100

*73. For the wife: Zones of the body when stimulated by your husband which give you the most sexual arousal (omit the clitoris) such as ears, lips, neck, breasts, back, thighs, etc.? List first, second, and third in order of the degree of arousal.

	1st	2nd	3rd	Weighted Total**
Breasts	62.3%	27.2%	10.5%	173
Lips	18.8%	27.0%	19.2%	88
Thighs	11.6%	14.0%	22.8%	77
Neck	2.9%	17.0%	26.3%	45
Ears	2.9%	10.0%	15.7%	29
Back	1.4%	.4%	5.3%	12

74. Do you communicate with each other during the sexual arousal period?

      7.0% None   67.6% A little   25.3% Considerable

75. Concerning the use of artificial lubrication:

    14.9% We have never needed to use artificial lubrication.

    48.6% We used to use it some, but we do not use it any more.

     2.7% We use artificial lubrication to stimulate the clitoris, but do not use any for intercourse.

    33.8% We use artificial lubrication both for stimulation of the clitoris and in intercourse.

76. Concerning birth control:

    54.8% We have never experimented with the "free period" method when we really did not want a pregnancy at that time.

    45.2% We have experimented some with the "free period" method when we really did not want a pregnancy at that time.

77. Have you practiced "coitus interruptus" (withdrawal before orgasm)?

    68.1% none   30.4% some   1.5% often

78. Concerning the use of contraceptives:

     6.0% We have never used contraceptives.

    54.0% We use contraceptives regularly and carefully.

    40.0% We use contraceptives most of the time, but have run risks.

79. Percent of contraceptives purchased by husband?

    86.1%

  Percent of contraceptives purchased by wife?

    13.9%

80. Before your marriage, was the wife's menstrual period?

    52.6% regular   34.6% slightly irregular

    12.8% very irregular

81. Since marriage, other than during pregnancy interruptions, has her menstrual period been?
    56.1% regular   39.9% slightly irregular
    4.0% very irregular

82. The menstrual period was present on our wedding day.
    Yes 17.0%   No 83.0%

83. Immediately after your marriage (assuming no immediate pregnancy) was the first menstrual period on time, early, or late?
    62.8% on time
    For 11.7% the period was an average of 4.3 days early.
    For 25.5% the period was an average of 5.6 days late.

84. Before marriage, did the wife have "cramps" connected with her menstrual period?
    17.3% none   63.3% some   19.3% extreme

85. Since marriage, menstrual "cramps" have been:
    15.5% none   72.3% some   12.2% extreme

86. Sex relations and the menstrual period: (check those that apply)
    27.7% We have avoided all sex relations during the menstrual period.
    18.1% We do not have sexual intercourse but do bring each other to orgasms during the menstrual period.
    41.9% We have had sexual intercourse during the period a few times, but we tend to have some reservations about it.
    12.3% Since most physicians insist that there can be no biological harm, we go ahead without reservations.

87. A few women have what is called "mid-month" pains, that is, pains at the ovulation period when the egg leaves the ovary. Does the wife have these mid-month pains?
    52.5% never   38.0% sometimes   9.5% regularly

88. Concerning the wife's sexual desire and the menstrual cycle: (check either a or b)

  a. 29.1% The degree of intensity is about the same during the entire cycle. It changes very little.

  b. 70.9% The degree of intensity changes during the cycle.

  For those who checked "b," it is high and low during the following times:

High	Low	
32.5%	17.9%	A few days before the menstrual period.
22.5%	21.2%	During the menstrual period.
33.1%	9.9%	A few days after the menstrual periods.
24.5%	13.2%	Halfway between the menstrual periods.

89. Other factors (such as responsibility, fatigue, the problems of the day, etc.) actually affect the wife's sexual desire more than the time of the menstrual cycle.

    Yes 85.6%   No 14.4%

90. There is a conflict of opinion about the part the clitoris and the vagina play in female orgasms. (Check all that apply to you.)

    39.1% The orgasm is located largely in the clitoris.

    4.6% It is located largely in the vagina.

    9.9% It is located equally in both.

    46.4% Located in both, but the clitoris is more pronounced.

    7.9% Located in both, but the vagina is more pronounced.

    66.2% The clitoris is the trigger setting off the orgasm.

    6.0% The vagina is the trigger.

91. When under sexual stimulation, does the clitoris increase in size?

    8.2% None

    67.4% Little

    22.2% Considerable

    2.2% Much

92. Some books state that the female orgasm is located in and involves the total body from the top of the head to the bottom of the feet.
    16.3% Agree fully
    37.0% Agree
    36.3% Not sure
    8.9% Disagree
    1.5% Disagree fully

*93. Do you have intercourse now (as compared with the first month of married life)?
    5.8% More often
    60.9% Less often
    33.3% About the same

*94. When intercourse and orgasms are finished, how soon do you withdraw?
    4.0% Immediately
    46.0% 1-2 minutes
    30.0% 3-4 minutes
    20.0% 5 minutes or longer

*95. After withdrawal, do you?
    58.8% Get up immediately and wash
    41.2% Have endearing conversation for several minutes?

*96. After your sexual experience at night, who goes to sleep first?
    38.0% Husband
    9.9% Wife
    52.1% Both about the same time

97. Rate your feeling about personal sexual satisfaction up to now.

	Husband	Wife
Excellent	58.5%	44.9%
Good	32.6%	36.8%
Average	7.4%	14.1%
Fair	1.5%	2.9%
Poor	0.0%	0.7%

98. What would the wife advise a married woman to do who has been married a year or more and has not achieved orgasm? Think this through thoroughly and give a careful reply.

    64% See a marriage counselor.

    62% See your family doctor.

    33% More relaxation and concentration.

    16% Have a long frank talk with husband.

    11% A longer period of direct stimulation.

*The questions marked by an asterisk were asked to only the last 80 of the 151 couples in the sample.
**First choice was weighted 3, second choice was weighted 2 and the third choice was weighted 1.

APPENDIX III

Some Suggestions to Pastors and Other Church Counselors

The churches of a community, with (1) their close ties to the family and (2) their Christian concepts concerning marriage and family life, have an ideal situation for an efficient pre-marriage and marriage counseling program. Although the responsibilities of pastors are legion, most pastors feel that pre-marriage counseling is their responsibility. This is at it should be. In some cases the pastor may want to delegate some of the responsibility to his wife, his educational director, some member of the church staff, or some other leader in the church membership such as a doctor, a social worker, or a teacher. The pastor may want to use a church "Christian Life" committee to help him lead out in the area of counseling. If he delegates counseling responsibility, he will need to be careful to select those leaders in his church who have the proper attitude and personality. He would want to train these persons thoroughly for this important aspect of church life. The following suggestions for pastors are concerned with the general sex education of youth, as well as a formal pre-marriage and marriage counseling conference.

I. Pre-marriage counseling should begin with the training of the parents of children ages 1-8 on "how to talk to their children about sex." The pastor's wife or some other qualified person in the church should be trained for this responsibility. There is abundant literature on this subject. See Appendix IV. Once every year or two the pastor's wife could lecture to a called meeting of these parents. At the meeting, some literature could be distributed to them. In this approach, Christianity and the Church can be associated with the subject of sex in the thinking of the child from the very beginning. The young parents of the church will welcome this information.

II. The church should plan separate meetings of the girls (ages 9-12) with their mothers, and of the boys ages 9-12 with their fathers for a film and/or lecture on sex education. Illustrative charts could be used. These meetings should be designed to prepare the boys and girls for the onset of puberty. There is an advantage of having children and their parents hear this type of lecture together. It will tend to promote free parent-child discussion on the subject. Most parents will welcome this type of meeting, sponsored by the church. This lecture could be given by the pastor to the boys and by the pastor's wife to the girls, or some other responsible church leader could be assigned this duty. Careful preparation is a "must" for those who lead these meetings. Literature and possible films or slides may be secured from denominational agencies.

III. A similar meeting should be held for the young people (ages 13 and up) of the church. The age division of all of the above meetings could be adjusted to fit the needs of each specific church. These meetings can be planned and carried out through the use of the existing organizational missionary, or some other county or divisional denominational leader who could specialize in these lectures and assist smaller churches in this sex education training.

IV. By careful planning in his preaching and teaching, a pastor can fuse Christian theology and a Christian interpretation of sexuality. He can lead all ages in his congregation to a wholesome level of thinking about the purpose and nature of marriage and sexuality. A pastor should be careful to distinguish between (1) the use of sex in marriage as planned by the Creator and (2) the misuse and abuse of sex as practiced by promiscuous immoral persons. In describing the latter, it is necessary to use such words as lust, adultery, fornication, lasciviousness, etc., but a pastor would need to be certain that the children and youth in his audience identified this language with the abuse of sex and *not* with sex as such. All negative statements about sex (and these are necessary) should be followed by positive statements about the purpose and significance of sex as planned by the Creator. In his positive message, a pastor should be frank, using exact and simple language, yet using it with Christian dignity.

V. A pastor should encourage the parents of his congregation to be positive as well as negative, when teaching their children regarding sex. It is normal for parents to warn their children about the dangers of sexual promiscuity. Such warnings are necessary. However, if each warning is followed by some positive ideas related to the place of sex in the Christian life, it will assist youth in developing healthy attitudes toward life and it will tend to develop a healthy parent-child relationship. Skillful pastoral leadership can be a bulwark of strength to the parents and children of a congregation in the area of sexual maturity.

VI. A pastor ought to plan a thorough pre-marriage counseling routine and inform his congregation about its nature and availability. Proper pre-marriage counseling would involve a series of conferences between the pastor and the bride and groom. One conference would plan details concerning the wedding ceremony. A second conference would involve instructions in the religious and spiritual nature of marriage and husband-wife relationships. There might be further conferences on some other aspects of marriage. Certainly there should be a final conference in which the pastor would give the couple some substantial help in the area of sexual adjustment in marriage. This type of help has been notoriously neglected far too long by many otherwise efficient pastors. This book is designed specifically, to assist pastors to give this help in a Christian frame of reference. The nature of this conference could be varied as follows.

1. The pastor might give the couple a copy of this book before their wedding day and instruct them to read, individually, Chapters 2 through 6.

2. It might be better for a pastor to have the couple come to his office or his home and have them read the book audibly, together, under his supervision.

3. It might be more efficient for the pastor and/or his wife at the church or in the pastor's home to read Chapters 2 through 6 from the book to the couple and allow them to ask questions at the end of each chapter.

4. Better still, the pastor and/or his wife could meet the couple privately at the church or at the pastor's home and give them orally, a thorough discussion of the details of Chapters 2 through 6. Although this would involve much time and energy, this personal touch would be an exceedingly valuable service to any young couple standing on the threshold of marriage. For a couple to read a book on the sexual aspect of marriage is good indeed, but they cannot ask a book a question, and receive an answer. "Books . . . are not substitutes for secure personal understandings with your pastor. . . ."[1]

All of these conferences would begin with prayer

and would be conducted in a relaxed atmosphere to demonstrate to the couple, the normal Christian attitude concerning the relationship between the spiritual and the sexual in marriage. Some arrangement should be made to give the couple this book to take on their honeymoon and to become a permanent part of their future library.

Notes

[1]Wayne E. Oates, *Where to Go For Help* (Philadelphia: The Westminster Press, 1957), p. 50.

APPENDIX IV

A Selected Bibliography

The following bibliography lists forty books that give further help on "sexual happiness in marriage." All these books are written from a Christian point-of-view with the exception of the last three, which are technical books, written for professionals only. Readers may purchase or order any or all of these books from religious bookstores, or they may be ordered directly from the publisher.

I. New Books That Relate Sex to General Husband-Wife Relationships

Christenson, Larry. *The Christian Family*. Minneapolis: Bethany Fellowship, 1974.

Dobson, James. *What Wives Wish Husbands Knew About Women*. Wheaton, Ill.: Tyndale House, 1975.

Drakeford, John W. *Made for Each Other*. Nashville: Broadman Press, 1973.

Hancock, Maxine. *Love, Honor and Be Free* (A Christian woman's response to today's call for liberation). Chicago: Moody Press, 1975.

Hollis, Harry, Jr. *Thank God for Sex*. Nashville: Broadman Press, 1975.

Hunt, Gladys. *Ms. Means Myself* (Being a woman in an uneasy world). Grand Rapids, Mich.: Zondervan Publishing House, 1972.

Jewett, Paul K. *Man as Male and Female*. Grand Rapids, Mich.: Wm. B. Eerdmans Publishing Company, 1975.

Landorf, Joyce. *Tough and Tender, What Every Woman Wants in a Man*. Old Tappan, N. J.: Fleming H. Revell Company, 1975.

Lovett, E. S. *The Compassionate Side of Divorce*. Old Tappan, N. J.: Fleming H. Revell Company, 1975.

Miles, Judith M. *The Feminine Principle*. Minneapolis: Bethany Fellowship, 1975.

Petersen, J. Allan, editor. *For Men Only*. Wheaton, Ill.: Tyndale House, 1975.

——————. *For Women Only*. Wheaton, Ill.: Tyndale House, 1975.

——————. *The Marriage Affair*. Wheaton, Ill.: Tyndale House, 1971.

Scanzoni, Letha, and Hardesty, Nancy. *All We're Meant To Be*. Waco, Tex.: Word Books, 1975.

Schaeffer, Edith. *What Is a Family?* Old Tappan, N. J.: Fleming H. Revell Company, 1975.

Sergio, Lisa. *Jesus and Woman*. EMP Publications, 1975.

Small, Dwight H. *Christian Celebrate Your Sexuality*. Old Tappan, N. J.: Fleming H. Revell Company, 1975.

II. Theological Books on Marriage and Sexuality

Bailey, Derrick S. *The Mystery of Love and Marriage*. New York: Harper and Brothers, 1952.

Feucht, Oscar E., editor. *Sex and the Church*. St. Louis: Concordia Publishing House, 1961.

Howell, John C. *Teachings About Sex*. Nashville: Broadman Press, 1966.

Piper, Otto A. *The Biblical View of Sex and Marriage*. New York: Charles Scribner's Sons, 1960.

White, Ernest. *Marriage and the Bible*. Nashville: Broadman Press, 1965.

III. Books on How to Teach Children and Young People About Sex

Child Study Association of America. *How to Tell Your Children About Sex*, revised edition. New York: Simon and Schuster, 1970.

Grant, Wilson W. *From Parent to Child About Sex*. Grand Rapids, Mich.: Zondervan Publishing House, 1973.

Howell, John C. *Teaching Your Children About Sex*. Nashville: Broadman Press, 1973

Kolf, Erwin J. *Parents Guide to Christian Conversation About Sex*. St. Louis: Concordia Publishing House, 1967.

Miles, Herbert J. *Sexual Understanding Before Marriage*. Grand Rapids, Mich.: Zondervan Publishing House, 1971.

Narramore, Clyde M. *How to Tell Your Child About Sex*. Grand Rapids, Mich.: Zondervan Publishing House, 1958.

Simmons, Paul D., and Crawford, Kenneth. *Growing Up With Sex*. Nashville: Broadman Press, 1973.

IV. Books on Sex Related to Courtship and Marriage

Fitch, William. *Christian Perspectives on Sex and Marriage*. Grand Rapids, Mich.: Wm. B. Eerdmans Publishing Company, 1971.

Mace, David R. *Whom God Hath Joined*. Philadelphia: Westminster Press, 1953.

Miles, Herbert J. *The Dating Game*. Grand Rapids, Mich.: Zondervan Publishing House, 1975.

Morgan, Marabel. *The Total Woman*. Old Tappan, N. J.: Fleming H. Revell Company, 1973.

Vincent, M. O. *God Sex and You*. New York: J. B. Lippincott, 1971.

Wheat, Ed. *Sex Problems and Sex Technique in Marriage* (A three-hour cassette series). 130 N. Spring St., Springdale, Ark., 1975.

V. GENERAL COLLEGE TEXTBOOKS ON FAMILY LIFE
WHICH INCLUDE EXCELLENT MATERIALS
ON HUMAN SEXUALITY

Bowman, Henry A. *Marriage for Moderns*, 6th edition. New York: McGraw-Hill, 1974.

Landis, Judson T., and Landis, Mary G. *Building a Succeesful Marriage*, 6th edition. Englewood Cliffs, N.J.: Prentice-Hall, 1974.

VI. SEX TEXTBOOKS WRITTEN FOR PROFESSIONALS ONLY

Kaplan, Helen Singer. *The New Sex Therapy*. New York: Brunner-Mazel Publishers, 1974. Actual treatment of sexual dysfunctions; written for professionals only. It does not follow a Christian point-of-view, but does come to grips with sexual problems.

Masters, William H., and Johnson, Virginia E. *Human Sexual Response*. Boston: Little, Brown and Company, 1966. Written for professionals only. It does not follow a Christian point-of-view, but does come to grips with human sexual problems.

_____. *Human Sexual Inadequacy*. Boston: Little, Brown and Company, 1970. Written for professionals only. It does not follow a Christian point-of-view, but does come to grips with human sexual inadequacy.

APPENDIX V

How to Locate a Qualified Marriage Counselor

1) A couple in need of a marriage counselor should go first to their own pastor. If the pastor is a qualified marriage counselor, he will give thorough and understanding counsel. If he is not, he will be the first to say so, and he will know how to help locate a marriage counselor. His advice will be dependable.

2) If for any reason, a couple feels they cannot go to their pastor, the next logical step is to write the American Association of Marriage and Family Counselors and ask for the name and location of one or more marriage counselors in their geographical area. That address is

American Association of Marriage
and Family Counselors
225 Yale Avenue
Claremont, California 91711

3) If a couple cannot locate a member of the American Association of Marriage and Family Counselors in their area, the next logical step is to contact a local family social service agency. In larger cities there are private family agencies, sometimes called Children's Bureaus, that give professional help in marriage counseling. Most social workers are not professional marriage counselors. Yet, most all family social service agencies will have a qualified marriage counselor on their staff.

If there is no private family service agency in the area, the couple could ask for help at the local County or City Social Welfare Office or mental health clinic.